# GARDEN RESCUE

# GARDEN RESCUE

**RICHARD BISGROVE**

FRANCES LINCOLN LIMITED
PUBLISHERS

Frances Lincoln Limited
4 Torriano Mews
Torriano Avenue
London NW5 2RZ
www.franceslincoln.com

A catalogue record for this book is available
from the British Library.

ISBN 10: 0-7112-2645-8
ISBN 13: 978-0-7112-2645-6

Printed and bound in the United Kingdom

9 8 7 6 5 4 3 2 1

# Contents

# Introduction

Two extremes of problem garden will be readily visualized by all garden owners: the new garden: a bare, flat, draughty patch of brickbat-ridden clay completely lacking shelter or privacy and the larger, neglected garden of an older house, a tangle of lilac suckers, laurels and dusty conifers interlaced with ivy, brambles and nettles with a liberal sprinkling of broken bottles, old mattresses and prams.

It would be possible and perhaps quite useful, to deal with these two extremes in turn but there are few gardens entirely free of problems – shady, dry, root-filled corners beneath trees, poorly drained hollows, neglected lawns or borders which, despite careful attention to routine cultivation, have outgrown their allotted space.

To deal with these problems is the objective of this small book. In order to make it more generally useful it is organized problem by problem rather than garden by garden and the problems are divided into five major categories: climate, (including microclimate, shade, exposure and related problems); difficult soils; garden dereliction; overgrown plants; and lawns.

Unfortunately, problems in the garden are never so distinct and clearly defined. Each problem is unique and a stereotyped solution is neither possible nor desirable. For this reason each section of the book begins with some general background information – on characteristics of windbreaks, on the nature and structure of soils, on the development of lawns – before dealing with specific solutions for specific problems. When appropriate, lists of plants are given for 'problem situations' but these lists are short and selective in nature, not encyclopaedic. Longer lists may be obtained from sources recommended in the last pages of the book. Only by working from the general to the particular and understanding the nature of a problem before looking for solutions is it possible to arrive at intelligent and appropriate answers to the infinite number of garden problems which present themselves.

It might be useful, also, to say what this book is not. It is not a manual of routine cultivation practices. It does not explain how to dig or sow, how to make a lawn or a vegetable garden. There are innumerable books which serve this purpose already. Nor does it discuss routine pruning operations, the cutting back to three buds or taking out old wood which is intended to produce bigger and better flowers. Instead it is directed to non-routine practices, to the creation of new gardens or restoration and reclamation of older ones.

To a considerable degree the great mass of general gardening books has helped to create many of the problems dealt with here. Most of our contemporary gardening habits are still based on the nineteenth-century concept of the 'gardenesque', a concept which, in its hackneyed twenty-first-century guise, over-emphasizes the routine cultivation of individual plants and under-emphasizes the importance of the garden as a whole. Most twentieth-century garden lore, whether in books or on the television, feeds on the notion of a garden as containing a stereotypical menu of garden features: the rose garden, the rock garden, the lily pond and pergola, the woodland walk and the kitchen garden etc. Many of the ingredients of this menu are assumed to require a deep, rich, moist but well-drained loam in an open, sunny situation. When, after years of trying to meet this ideal by cutting everything back to three buds or seasoning the borders with well-rotted stable manure or leafmould, the roses fail, the rhododendrons are anaemic and our hundred metre depth of heavy clay is not transformed into deep, rich, moist but well-drained loam, there is no solace to be derived. Overgrown borders, clay soil and any other departure from the stereotype are defined as problems rather than as idiosyncracies.

It is now fifty years since the American landscape architect Thomas Church first published *Gardens are for People*, encouraging a more pragmatic, user-focused approach to garden making but much of the English garden information industry has yet to catch up with his ideas.

*Garden Rescue* is intended as an antidote to the more straightforward and dogmatic treatises on gardening. Pruning should be seen not solely in relation to the needs of individual plants but as a means of shaping the garden in general, and thus it is treated in Chapter 4). Clay soil is only a problem if one insists on trying to grow plants (including fine lawns) which require deep, well-drained etc., etc.

In a way the book offers a reinterpretation of problems rather than a solution. One could say that there is no such thing as a problem garden, only problem gardeners with misguided and unrealistic expectations. Certainly very heavy or very light soils, very exposed or very shady situations limit the range of plants which can be grown but they also allow a whole range of other plants to flourish, making it possible to create gardens of distinctive and varied character. When these 'difficult' conditions are seen as constraints guiding the development of the garden rather than as problems preventing its cultivation by traditional means for traditional ends, the work of creating and maintaining a garden is greatly eased. The garden will take on its own character, appropriate to its surroundings, without profligate expenditure of time, effort and materials.

Nineteenth-century gardening practices and garden styles evolved when large armies of paid staff were commonplace and it is these traditions which are still perpetuated in much current gardening literature. Times have changed: the employment of large numbers of skilled professional gardeners is no longer feasible and our ideas of what constitutes a satisfying garden are also changing. A new sort of book is needed to help the twenty-first-century gardener – the unpaid and self-employed enthusiast – and I hope that *Garden Rescue* will help to meet this need.

# 1. Climate, Exposure and Shade

It is climate which ultimately determines the uses to which the garden can be put, whether use is thought of in terms of growing plants or of accommodating people. The study of climate, therefore, can be very rewarding when making a garden. It pays to remember, however, that 'climate' is a long-term simplification of 'weather', an element so quixotic as to provide an infallible topic of conversation for the traditionally taciturn Englishman. Severe cold, drought, heatwaves or floods *can* occur in our generally temperate climate and may cause havoc, especially in adventurously planted gardens, and increasingly apparent signs of climate change will challenge all gardeners.

Climate may be considered on a variety of scales, from international to local. On a world scale Britain has a temperate maritime climate. Although there are occasional extremes, one remembers the bitter winter of 1962–3, the drought of 1976, the storms of 1987 and 1990 and the floods of recent years as exceptions to the usual not-very-hot, not-very-cold and rather damp weather to which we are accustomed. Our unremarkable climate has enabled grass to grow extremely well, so lawns are taken very much for granted; it also enables us to cultivate plants introduced from many parts of the world, but for this one needs to look more closely at variations within Britain.

## REGIONAL CLIMATE

In the very simplest regional terms the north of Britain is colder than the south; the east is drier than the west. However, Britain is a small, bumpy island and this simple pattern of latitude and longitude is greatly modified by a third factor, the mollifying effect of the sea. Because of the enormous heat store which the ocean represents, coastal areas are cooler in summer and warmer in winter than are areas a kilometre or two inland. This effect is particularly marked on the west coast where the deeply indented coastline is washed by the warm waters of the North Atlantic Drift, or Gulf Stream. Given protection from Atlantic gales which also sweep the west coast, this mildness makes possible such enchanting gardens as Tresco in the Scilly Isles, Bodnant in North Wales and Inverewe, in which palm trees and other tender plants flourish at a latitude north of Moscow or the lower Hudson Bay.

Largely because of the sea's influence, a mere 3°C (5°F) separate the mean temperatures of northern Scotland and southern England, whether in winter or summer. Rainfall varies more widely, 550–600mm (21–23in) in East Anglia, 650–750mm (25–30in) in much of eastern England and 1,150–1,250mm (45–50in) in the west with two or three times as much falling in small upland areas along the west coast. On the whole, regional differences are not large, certainly not comparable with the ten climatic zones into which the United States is divided, from arctic Alaska to subtropical Florida. Nevertheless, the variation is sufficient to impress a general regional character on our gardens and to offer broad generalization as to the types of plants which may be grown satisfactorily.

**The north-west**
The north-west is relatively mild and humid. Given protection from the prevailing westerly winds, hardy rhododendrons and their allies grow to perfection and, because of the constant moisture, primulas, trilliums and other plants from woodland habitats flourish in the open, flowering more freely in the improved light conditions. *Tropaeolum speciosum*, which merely tolerates other regions if it survives at all, here romps through gardens at an embarrassing rate and flowers in general show up brilliantly against the cool, watery sky.

### The south-west
Many of these same plants thrive in the south-west, but the
further south one goes, the more safely can one add to the list
more tender plants: embothriums, pittosporums, acacias, tree
ferns, palms and the large-leaved rhododendrons. Not only is
the climate favourable for growth but it is usually free from
frosts which might otherwise damage flowers of the earliest
rhododendrons, camellias and magnolias.

### The south-east
The climate of the south-east is drier and less equable. Higher
summer temperatures and cold winters, sometimes with heavy
falls of snow, favour many North American plants adapted to a
continental rather than a maritime climate. *Sassafras, Cornus
florida* and other trees of the eastern United States ripen wood
more satisfactorily than in the more humid west and autumn
colour is enhanced. Most grey-leaved plants also flourish in the
south-east on well-drained soils, but some are tender and are
damaged more by the cold east winds of this region than by
the higher rainfall of the west.

### The north-east
Low temperatures and low rainfall in the north-east combine
to produce a climate politely termed 'bracing'. It is not
conducive to plant growth or physical comfort but, especially at
higher altitudes and away from coastal fogs, it does make
possible the cultivation of many high alpine plants which
would be considered extremely difficulty in other parts of the
country. This is not to say that other plants will not grow, of
course, but gardeners would be advised to choose the hardier
types and to expect slower growth rates.

## LOCAL CLIMATE

In our small, irregular and windy island, local variations in climate are more marked and often more significant than regional differences.

### Orientation
A south or south-west facing slope or wall will trap the sun's energy and create a local climate equivalent to moving the garden several hundreds of kilometres further south. A sheltered garden in Yorkshire, for example, might grow plants found in the open in southern England; a sheltered garden in Kent or Hampshire might rival the botanical riches of the French riviera. The other side of the slope or wall will, of course, be commensurately disadvantaged, the problem being especially severe in the north where an adverse slope may receive no direct sunlight in winter and only weak light in high summer. Gardens in such conditions would be limited to ferns, ivies and other shade-tolerant plants or to the hardier forest trees.

### Wind
Wind is an important and unpredictable element in the garden climate. Coastal gardens and those in elevated positions invariably require some form of shelter from wind. Hills will often funnel and divert the wind through valleys so low-lying gardens are not invariably sheltered. In urban areas buildings, and especially tall buildings, cause eddying of the wind, adding to rather than reducing its force and exacerbating its damaging effect with flurries of dust and litter.

The effects of the wind are manifold. It can cause direct damage by snapping branches or bruising leaves; it increases water loss by evaporation and thus decreases temperature. The combination of cold, dry conditions reduces growth. Wind also carries disease spores, aphids and other pests from plant to plant and will reduce the activity of pollinating insects so vital early in the year to the later success of fruit crops. Thus sheltered areas are warmer and more humid: more comfortable for people, more conducive to plant growth and pollination but the advantage is not absolute. Windborne pests and diseases will settle out in sheltered zones and will also flourish more freely in the improved environment. Shelter may also imply shade, which causes soft, weak growth and, if the shelter is derived from a living hedge or tree belt, the competition for water and nutrients may outweigh any advantage of reduced evaporation. By reducing wind speed, a shelter belt can also increase the risk of radiation frost and create a frost pocket.

## Rainfall

Although variations of local climate are widely appreciated in terms of wind and temperature, the effect on rainfall is frequently overlooked. The amount of rain falling is determined by regional rather than local factors, but the droplets are diverted by wind and reach the ground in a very uneven distribution. In particular the soil against walls, even on the windward side, receives much less rain than falls in the open ground. The leeward side is drier still and overhanging eaves will exacerbate the inequality – unless, of course, the gutters leak, in which case a micro-environment of quite a different type will be created! Local unevenness of rainfall is of minor importance in the long term; plants exploit a large volume of soil and will seek out water supplies. It is very important, however, to make adequate preparation for new plants against walls. The soil should be well prepared, the plant put in away from the wall (and trained back to it if required) and watered generously for at least one summer, or two if the weather is exceptionally dry.

Even from these brief notes it should be apparent that climate is determined as much by what is on the ground as by what the air brings. To appreciate this one has only to walk across a black tarmac drive then over a sunny lawn to the shade of trees in summer, or to walk past a gap in a hedge on a windy winter's day. It follows, therefore, that much can be done in the making of a garden to create favourable conditions in which to enjoy it. This can be achieved by improving shelter and privacy and by providing some shade or, in the case of gardens already excessively shady, by planning the garden to minimize its adverse effects.

## COPING WITH EXPOSURE

The garden may be exposed physically to cold or strong winds or, less commonly in our usually damp island, to too much sun. It may also be exposed visually to the gaze of neighbours and passers-by, or to undesirable views. As the latter affects 'psychological comfort' in the garden as much as the former affects physical comfort, both can logically be dealt with under one main heading, the more so as the solutions to the two types of problem are very similar.

### Screening

The obvious answer to undue exposure is to erect a suitable screen, such a screen often serving many purposes. It may be required to break the force of the wind, to hide an eyesore, to create privacy, to add a decorative element to the garden or to provide more food.

As with all aspects of garden design it is important that any screen becomes part of the garden's general structure and is not 'plonked down' arbitrarily to serve a single function.

In the garden, the screen may be a wall, a fence, a line of plants (whether a 'hedge' in the narrow sense of the word or a less formal shrub border) or some combination of these three. Each has its advantages and disadvantages.

## Walls

Walls are immediately effective as screens and, if well built, will last for centuries with virtually no maintenance. They take up little ground space but are unfortunately exceedingly expensive.

## Fences

Fences also serve their screening function as soon as they are erected and may take even less ground space. They, too, require little maintenance and if their substantially lower cost must be measured against a lifespan counted in decades rather than centuries, the saving is usually considered worthwhile in an age in which a great many families move at least once in each generation. As the life of the fence depends very much on the durability of that part of it near the ground, the slight additional cost of raising the fence on reinforced concrete posts or metal bases is often amply justified.

## Trellis

Where a complete screen is neither necessary nor desirable, an open-work fence or trellis may be used. An open trellis will obscure the background and, by creating a subtle pattern of its own, can distract the eye from undesirable views beyond. Random or rhythmically spaced bars are most effective for this purpose but even a plain square pattern is useful. Prefabricated trellis panels, when opened out, have a diamond pattern which, although pleasing enough, has an irritating zigzag outline. These panels should be mounted in a strong frame to provide the necessary strength and simplicity of outline.

When trellis and climbing plants are to be used in conjunction it is important to decide which is the more important partner. A plain trellis serving only as a support may have such vigorous climbers as honeysuckle, *Clematis montana*, Russian vine or winter jasmine trained on it. A trellis intended to create a pattern in its own right should have lighter climbers –

*Clematis viticella, Eccremocarpus scaber* or perhaps a trained vine, while very elaborate patterns of treillage may be sufficient in themselves. Further suggestions for climbing plants are offered at the end of this chapter.

*Hedges*

Hedges, unlike walls and fences, must grow for several years before they become effective screens. They also require regular maintenance: shaping at least once and sometimes several times each year to encourage dense growth in the early years and to keep the plants within bounds subsequently. At maturity a hedge is seldom less than half a metre in width, often more, representing a substantial loss of space in small gardens. The hedge will also require adequate water and nutrients, competing with nearby plants for these essentials.

Set against these problems, however, are some very significant advantages. Firstly, the initial expenditure can be quite slight, especially if small plants are purchased and planted by the garden owner. Furthermore, hedges or other shrub plantings will be selected to beautify the garden and therefore can sensibly be counted as additions to rather than subtractions from it. If shelter from wind is an important consideration, the most important virtue of a hedge is that it is a much stronger and more efficient windbreak than is a solid wall or fence. Freak gales which might expensively flatten whole lengths of wall or fence will often cause only minor loss of leaves and twigs from a hedge which can bend before the wind – and even this loss is made good by the plants at no cost to the owner! The aerodynamics of hedges are further explained on pages 21–2.

**Siting a screen**

Whatever kind of screen is required, it is important to bear in mind a few simple, but often forgotten, points.

The nearer the screen is to the site to be sheltered, the less height is required to achieve the necessary protection. A few

fence panels immediately around a terrace will create an intimate sheltered corner permanently or just until a more distant
screening hedge gains the necessary stature. Fencing within
(rather than around) the garden also provides an opportunity
to conceal parts of the garden either for introducing an
element of surprise or, more practically, for concealing compost
heaps, vegetable gardens and washing lines. Changes in level
offer even more opportunity. A sunken terrace, perhaps
surrounded by a retaining wall just high enough for sitting on,
will need only a low hedge of rosemary, potentilla, heather,
etc., to create complete privacy without interfering with views
from the house. Bends in a wall or fence add greatly to its
strength. Wrapping a fence around two or three sides of a
terrace not only makes it much easier to support but helps to
tie the fence into the garden as a whole. Whereas a line of
fence panels looks like a temporary and flimsy screen, an alcove
of fence panels becomes part of the ground plan of the garden.

## Screening for privacy

Visual exposure is a very common problem in new gardens.
Where complete privacy is essential, a solid wall or fence will
be required. In this case woven fence panels provide an effective solution: they are cheaper than vertical close-board
fencing, though less durable, and create a pleasantly coloured
and textured background without being too obvious. However,
solid walls or fences result in poor air circulation and gusty
eddies of wind, as well as unduly confining the eye in a small

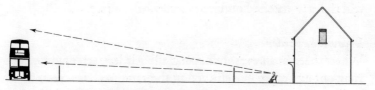

A fence near the house makes a more effective
screen than one at the other end of the garden.

garden, so a less claustrophobic enclosure is often desirable. A hedge, honeycomb or other decorative wall, slatted fence or trellis, with or without the embellishment of climbing plants, will achieve the required effect. A trellis with restrained climbers is especially effective in obscuring the view into and out of a garden while allowing light and air to penetrate. The trellis creates a pattern of shadows which add a delightful air of mystery to the garden.

## Hiding an ugly view

Blocking undesirable views from the garden may be as important as stopping people looking in, and again the type of screen needs to be carefully considered.

### Within the garden

When the eyesore is within the garden, perhaps a shed, garage or greenhouse, it is usually the hard outline and bulk which offend rather than the actual appearance of the building. In this case it is generally more satisfactory to soften the outline with plants behind the building, or to reduce the bulk by planting to cast shadows on it, than to attempt to hide it with a row of conifers, merely substituting one hard, bulky outline for another. If, on careful inspection, the building really does appear to be ugly, there are two possible lines of action: the problem can be solved by painting, repair or even demolition, or it can be hidden. In the latter case, rounded shrubs or small trees, a trellis with climbers or even complete immersion in a vigorous climber will provide a more satisfactory screen than will the saw-toothed outline of a row of conifers.

### Beyond the garden

When there is an eyesore beyond the garden, screening of the view out can often be achieved in the same way as screening of the view in for privacy, as discussed above. In some instances, however, attempts to obliterate the view are futile. Gas works, pylons, high-rise buildings and other giants of the skyline will not retreat behind a woven fence or a row of apple trees. It *is* possible to conceal the ground-level clutter of vehicles, cables, pipes and so on with a visual screen, leaving simple, large shapes which are dramatic even if not gardenesque. Soft, billowing plants breaking the vertical lines of the large shape and framing views of it will succeed surprisingly well in subduing the giant feature, which can then be used, when appropriate, as a background for trees or shrubs: silver-leaved pear or winter-flowering cherry against a dark building, for example, or purple birch, maples or cotinus against a grey-green gas holder.

If none of these techniques will produce the required effect, it may be desirable to turn the garden round. One tends to think automatically of a house leading across a terrace to the garden but, if the outlook is unsuitable, a terrace at the far end of the garden can have delightful advantages. It has the aspect opposite to that of the house, so there is always a choice of sun or shade. Attractive furniture and bright pots of flowers against a dark hedge will provide a strong focal point to distract from the more distant eyesore and the view from the terrace will be across the garden to the house, which can always be made attractive by framing or softening with plants. Overhead canopies, whether trees, pergolas or other frameworks, will also focus the view on objects nearer the ground, making it easier to obscure tall eyesores as well as providing welcome shade in summer.

## Protecting from the sun

Exposure to sun may not strike Britons as an obvious problem, but south-facing picture windows can render a room unbearably hot and cause the fading of curtains, carpets and furniture. In the garden, too, if the weather is conducive to being outside it is frequently too hot to stay for very long: apart from avid sun-worshippers we enjoy sunshine most from a slightly shaded position. Shade also intensifies flower colours, and the varied patterns of light and shade create many delightful garden effects. In winter, of course, every ray of sunshine is cherished, but by thoughtful use of plants it is possible to have the best of both worlds.

A light overhead framework of timber supporting a climbing plant or two will provide just the right dappled shade and, correctly positioned, will shade from the fierce midsummer while allowing low winter light to flood into the house. A loggia, summerhouse or arbour positioned to shade from midday sun can also trap the setting sun and soften the chill breeze which might otherwise drive one inside. Such a sheltered alcove pointing towards a pool, statue or other feature and surrounded by scented plants can create a world in itself amidst the least promising surroundings.

For overhead trellis, the pendant flowers of wisteria and laburnum or the bold leaves, hanging bunches of fruit and translucent autumn colour of the vines are ideal. All of these are pruned hard in winter and cast a minimum of shadow. Roses, clematis and other popular flowers are less satisfactory: they flower most freely above the trellis where they can be appreciated only from bedroom windows.

When man-made trellis would be too formal or too over-bearing, trees can be used to create their own structures. Gleditsia, robinia, acacia (in sheltered areas), *Prunus subhirtella* and birch quickly create light shade but eventually become large trees. *Gleditsia triacanthos* 'Sunburst' and *Robinia pseudoacacia* 'Frisia,' both yellow-leaved, are slower and create their own sunshine on duller days. Gleditsia in particular comes into leaf after most other trees and the leaves colour and fall quite early in autumn, shading the garden only when shade is most valued. Other plants – *Aralia chinensis*, *Rhus typhina*, even lilac and mock orange – which are scarcely more than large shrubs can be pruned up to perform as small trees in less spacious gardens. When light in the house is of paramount importance, lower plants still can be planted above a sunken terrace to create a shaded corner of garden. *Magnolia* × *soulangeana*, *Hamamelis mollis*, *Acer palmatum* and *Sorbus sargentiana* are relatively slow-growing, spreading shrubs which can be shaped to make a low canopy. They are always pleasant and at some time spectacular – in flower, fragrance, autumn colour or winter outline.

## Shelter from the wind

Exposure to wind is a more common problem than is generally realized. In coastal and elevated gardens, provision of shelter may be an absolute prerequisite before any other gardening activity can be contemplated. Even in less exposed areas, however, shelter from wind will usually improve the garden climate and enable more use to be made of the garden.

As with visual exposure, the solution is to erect a screen, but there are two important differences. Firstly, for a wind shelter a permeable barrier is much better than a solid barrier. Solid barriers cause air turbulence and create eddies which are often more damaging than the unabated wind. More open fences or pierced walls abate the force of the wind but allow some air to pass through, stabilizing the air-stream and producing a deeper zone of calmer air. Plants provide the best windbreaks. They not only deflect the wind but, by bending leaves and twigs, absorb some of its energy. Where wind is a serious problem, plants or perforated screens should invariably be selected in preference to solid walls or fences. The second difference is that, whereas light travels in straight lines, and so the effect of a screen on views or shading can be calculated precisely, the wind varies in force and direction from moment to moment; it moves over and around obstructions so the effect of a wind-break is less clear-cut, especially in built-up areas where the wind pattern is complicated by eddying and turbulence.

In general, however, the effectiveness of a windbreak depends on its height, not on its thickness. A well-furnished hedge will offer slight protection for a distance up to ten times its height to windward and thirty times its height to leeward. More significantly, the wind speed is reduced by half or more for a short distance to windward and for ten times the height of the hedge to leeward. For example, a 2m (6ft) high hedge will create a sheltered zone for 20m (60ft) behind it, and a single 10m (30ft) high windbreak will shelter 100m (300ft), as much land as five 2m (6ft) high hedges spaced 20m (60ft) apart.

## Windbreaks for the garden

The function of a windbreak must be considered in determining its siting and nature. If shelter is required for the whole garden the choice lies between a single tall boundary hedge and several lower internal divisions. Which is preferable will depend entirely on the size of the garden and its overall design. Sheltering the house, greenhouse and other buildings can

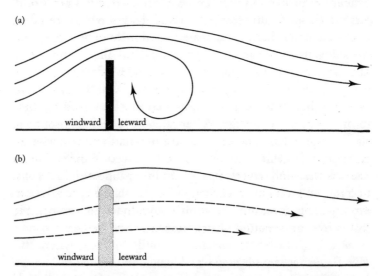

A solid wall obstructs air movement and causes fierce, damaging eddies (a).
A hedge absorbs and diffuses the wind's energy to provide a deep zone of shelter (b).

result in substantial reduction in heating costs but will require a taller windbreak. Scattered trees or tree clumps will reduce wind speed to some extent but a complete belt of trees is more effective. It is important to remember, though, that a shelter belt allowed to become open at the base can result in increased, rather than reduced, wind speed at ground level.

The nature of protection required is also important. If winter winds are the main problem evergreen hedges are more effective than deciduous ones although too dense a hedge may be a disadvantage. Well-trimmed deciduous hedges such as hawthorn, berberis, beech, hornbeam and even privet (which retains some of its leaves) are very nearly as effective in winter as in summer while evergreen conifers may become too dense and function more as solid barriers. A walk through woodland in the winter is sufficient to demonstrate the effectiveness of bare trees in breaking the force of the wind, although this is a case of defence in depth, not suitable for most gardens. Maximum protection is given when the hedge lies perpendicular to the path of the wind, so wind direction must be taken into account. In Britain the strongest winds usually come from the south-west, so protection from physical damage from this direction will often be important, especially in the west of the country. The coldest winds, however, are from the north and east and the garden climate can be greatly improved by sheltering from these quarters. In coastal areas winds off the sea are most important, not only in strength and frequency but in carrying inland damaging quantities of salt. In hilly inland districts the wind may be funnelled into unexpected directions, but if the problem is sufficient to warrant urgent action, evidence of prevailing winds is usually apparent in the distorted growth patterns of existing trees and hedgerows.

### Windbreaks for the kitchen garden

In the kitchen garden shelter is required near the ground and permanent hedges might interfere with crop rotation and soil cultivation. Temporary windbreaks of hessian, wattle hurdles or even pea-sticks can be used in winter and, if wind protection is required in summer, intercropping can be invaluable. In commercial growing, strawberries are sometimes intercropped with a few rows of barley or wheat to prevent sandy soil from being blown away. The same shelter can be achieved in the vegetable garden by using peas or beans to shelter low crops, making sure, of course, that the pea or bean supports themselves are strong enough to withstand strong winds. Jerusalem artichokes also make a very useful windbreak, especially for new gardens. The tubers are prepared and eaten like potatoes (except that they are less easy to peel!), and enough tubers are usually left in the ground to establish a screen the next year – which may or may not be helpful. Espalier fruit trees offer an attractive means of creating more permanent shelter but the trees themselves need a reasonably sheltered environment to encourage pollinating insects. Raspberry rows are not so long-lived but are more quickly established. The structure of a fruit cage often lends itself to draping with additional netting for wind protection, and it can often be sited with advantage in the most exposed part of the garden whereas unprotected fruit trees on the exposed boundary may suffer from poor pollination.

## THE DISADVANTAGES OF SHELTER

### Avoiding frost pockets
Inevitably, conflicts will arise between the need for shelter and other considerations. The incidence of radiation frost is accentuated by reducing wind speed and preventing cold and warm air-layers from mixing. Cold air flows downhill and will pile up behind a windbreak, increasing frost damage. On sites where frost is a particular problem, indeed on sloping sites in general, it is important to site shelter belts in such a way as to divert cold air which would flow downhill into the garden, opening the lower boundaries to allow escape of cold air.

## Avoiding excessive shade

Shelter belts cast shade. Clearly one would not want to save heating bills by casting the house or greenhouse into perpetual gloom. However, shelter from cold winds is required mainly from the north, leaving the south aspect open and sunny. Even if shelter belts are necessary on the south side, perhaps to reduce gale damage, remember that the shelter effect extends ten times the height of the hedge, whereas midday shading, even in midwinter, extends only five times the height of the hedge, so sunlight and shelter are not incompatible.

## Preserving the view

Interference with a view is a common problem, especially on the coast or on hillsides where complete shelter may be achieved only by sacrificing fine views which may well have been the main reason for choosing the situation. Again, compromise is possible. One can shelter part of the garden in such a way as to frame the view. On a large scale this might be achieved with trees and shrub borders spaced like stage settings to baffle the wind from many directions without creating a wind funnel which would be worse than no shelter at all. On a smaller scale, trellis or hedges sheltering the garden may have windows cut in them to frame the best views. Changes in level may also be used to create sheltered parts of the garden without interrupting views from the house. In rare circumstances it may be essential to preserve an entire panorama while providing shelter. This can only be done by erecting a glass screen, after which one might be tempted to add shelter from rain and cold, in other words to retire inside from the garden. However, as panoramic sweeps are seldom as permanently satisfying as smaller, carefully framed vistas, one should think very carefully about the treatment of views before deciding on this solution.

## Effect on snow drift

Lastly among the more important conflicts of interest, inter-ference with wind flow will affect everything carried on the wind. The biological effects of windborne insects, wild flower seeds and so forth are too complex to be dealt with here. The effect of a windbreak on rainfall has already been mentioned under 'Local climate' (page 13), and I would reiterate the warning that plants near walls, fences or hedges should be chosen to suit the aspect and be given particular care during establishment. The effect of snowfall must also be discussed briefly. Like rain, snow falls unevenly, but drifting is affected by wind speed and quantity of snow as well as by the nature of the windbreak. With light winds and moderate snowfalls the main drift is a short distance to the leeward of the windbreak (south-west if the snow is carried on north-easterlies), so a drive along the base of the windbreak or 30m (100ft) from it will be free of drifting snow. However, as wind speed and snowfall increase, the drift moves nearer the windbreak and a drive along its base may be deeply buried. In practice, drifting of snow in small gardens is complicated by the presence of the house, shrubs, herbaceous plant stems and even the lawn. Even apart from this, it would be of little use to advise siting the drive 30m (100ft) from the hedge in a garden only 10m (30–35ft) wide! Only in areas of heavy snowfall when the property is of park rather than garden proportions is snow likely to be considered in the design. Owners of such proper-ties would be advised to consult the classic work on the subject, J. Caborn, *Shelterbelts and Windbreaks* (Faber, 1965), in which snow drifting is given detailed consideration.

### ESTABLISHMENT OF SCREENS

### Planting

All trees and shrubs anchor themselves and adjust themselves to hostile situations much more satisfactorily if planted when small than if transplanted as large 'instant' specimens. In the case of conifers, and especially pines, it is essential to plant only small seedlings if severe exposure is expected. For shrubs the planting size is less critical, but it is not advisable to plant pot-grown specimens in which roots have twined around the pot. Such plants should be discarded if seriously pot-bound. Less seriously affected plants should have the roots unravelled and spread out at planting. Alternatively, the root ball may be slit from top to bottom at three or four places around the ball to stimulate new roots to grow outwards. Care should also be taken when planting hedge materials which have been heeled in or machine planted at some stage, to avoid a one-sided and hence unstable root system.

**Preparation of the ground**
If the temptation to use 'instant' plants can be avoided, the money thus saved can be invested to much greater effect in thorough preparation of the ground and perhaps in the purchase of a few temporary plants or the erection of a temporary windbreak. In very light or heavy soils it is important not to improve only a narrow, clearly defined trench, as roots may confine themselves to this zone as effectively as if they were in a pot. On heavy soil, moreover, a narrow trench of prepared soil will act as a sump for drainage water and roots will be drowned.

Permanent shelter plants should not be staked. If plants start to lean the root system will develop to support the plant. A propped-up plant will fail to restore its balance in this way and will require more and more elaborate support until the task becomes impossible. Eucalyptus are notorious for growing upwards at a rate which exceeds the ability of the root system to support so these trees are best left to establish themselves for about three years then cut right to the ground. The stool which develops can be thinned to a single stem again if required, and will be more wind-firm as a result of the fresh start. Other broad-leaved trees which develop a lean early on in life may be treated in the same way. Conifers do not respond to such brutality. A lean which develops early on in the life of a hedge may be dealt with by replacing the leaning tree with a new small plant, carefully preparing the ground before planting. In older hedges the lean can only be allowed to develop until the tree falls – if safety permits – or is removed. The gap may then be filled by replanting (again after thorough ground preparation with perhaps a temporary fence to prevent wind roaring through the gap) or, usually more satisfactorily, by tying branches from adjacent trees across the gap.

When a screen is to be established in a very exposed situation, a temporary fence of hessian, wattle hurdles, split chestnut, bamboo or proprietary windbreak material will assist early growth while allowing the plants to become gradually accustomed to the full force of the wind as they outgrow their protection.

## Double planting

When using plants for screening purposes there is a major conflict between the desire for immediate effect and the need for permanence. Plants which grow quickly to the required size either continue to grow equally quickly thereafter, necessitating much maintenance to keep them in bounds, or are short-lived and will soon require replacement. Slower-growing and more durable plants are eminently satisfactory in the long term but few people are now able to wait decades for substantial hedges or woodland belts to make effective shelter, especially if a move is anticipated every five years or so.

Because of this conflict of requirements it is often desirable to use a combination of plants. On a large scale birch, willow or, in mild areas, eucalyptus will produce a rapid screen and nurse up beech, oak, ash and other durable trees. On a more modest scale, privet, *Lonicera nitida*, *Buddleia alternifolia*, *Spiraea* × *vanhouttei*, brooms and other quick-growing shrubs will create a temporary screen while beech, yew, hornbeam and other such desirable hedges become established. In this instance the permanent hedge should be planted where it is required (along the boundary, for example), while the temporary plants are used as an informal hedge or shrub border within the garden. In this way they will shelter the garden even more quickly by their close proximity, without interfering with the permanent hedge. Indeed, bearing in mind that some shelter is created even on the windward side of a hedge, the temporary may help in the establishment of the permanent hedge, so long as it is removed before it overfills the garden.

Even in the smallest garden, in which a climber-covered screen is to be used for shelter, such double planting can be invaluable. It is often forgotten that even vigorous climbers take some time to become established. Very often a clematis, rose, honeysuckle – even the rampant Russian vine – will produce one weak shoot in the first year, a few stronger shoots in the second and really begin to grow vigorously in the third or fourth year. These permanent screens can be given substance in the early years by planting annual climbers – hops, sweet peas, *Cobaea scandens*, passion flower (a perennial which may be grown as an annual) or even that useful and decorative climber, the runner bean. The thorough preparation of the ground which is essential to the success of annual climbers will also benefit the permanent plants and, although care must be taken to prevent the latter from being smothered, the danger is not as great as might be imagined. Woody perennial climbers, which already have a well-developed root system, grow vigorously in the first flush of spring and have largely ceased to grow by midsummer. Annuals, which must grow afresh each year from a small seed, do not really become established until midsummer, a time at which they are most valuable in the garden but least damaging to their perennial neighbours. Truly annual climbers will also usually exhaust themselves quite early in the autumn and can be removed to allow the perennials to ripen wood before the onset of winter.

When double planting is used, it is very important to pay attention first to the siting and care of the permanent plants. It is obviously not wise to crowd permanent and temporary plants together so that a thin, misshapen screen is all that remains in time. Especially where permanent shelter from strong or persistent wind is required, slow but sure must be the guiding principle.

## PLANTS FOR SCREENING

Choice of plants will depend on personal likes and dislikes, on soil, locality, aspect and many other factors. However, below are short and selective lists of some of the most suitable plants for screening purposes with very brief notes on their characteristics.

### Evergreen climbers
These are extremely varied in habit and requirements. They are generally less colourful in flower than their deciduous counterparts but may be more attractive in winter.

*Berberidopsis corallina* (coral plant): climbs by twining stems but may require tying. Spectacular plant with pendulous brilliant red flower clusters. Unfortunately not very hardy and, although technically evergreen, its leaves are a liability rather than an asset if damaged by winter weather; best in a very sheltered, rather shady situation on peaty soil.

*Clematis armandii*: climbs by twining leaf-stalks. Handsome, dark green leaves and scented white flowers in spring. Hardy, although leaves may scorch in severe weather; flowers most freely when it has reached the top of its support and begins to hang down, so do not prune hard.

*Clematis cirrhosa* var. *balearica* (*C. balearica*): climbs by twining leaf-stalks. Surprisingly little known plant with dissected glossy leaves becoming purple in winter; flowers small, white, spotted purple within and slightly fragrant, borne freely in winter.

*Euonymus fortunei radicans*: clings by aerial rootlets. The cream-edged *E.f.r.* 'Variegatus', the most widely used form, is usually seen as a low, spreading shrub as are the larger-leaved 'Silver Queen' and the newer, brighter 'Emerald 'n' Gold'. They will all cling to rough surfaces, however, and climb slowly to provide hardy cover in almost any soil or situation. *E.f.r.* 'Vegetus' is more vigorous with larger, pale, glossy green leaves. This form also flowers more freely than the others and bears bright orange and red 'spindle' fruits.

*Hedera helix* (ivy): clings to rough surfaces by aerial rootlets but may also be 'woven' through trellis, etc. This and other species of ivy make handsome climbing plants, especially in the shade where leaves develop an additional glossiness; there are many cut-leaved, crisped and variegated forms. All are slow to start climbing but gradually gain momentum. They grow more rapidly (and again more splendidly) if partially smothered in annual or deciduous climbers and when they reach the top of their supports will produce branched, flowering shoots.

*Hydrangea serratifolia*: clings by aerial rootlets. A distinguished and unusual climber superficially resembling a handsome ivy; the greenish-white inflorescences are produced in late summer and, although more interesting than beautiful, are a considerable addition to the plant.

*Lonicera japonica* (Japanese honeysuckle): climbs by twining stems. Although evergreen, the leaves are not especially decorative except in the variety *L.j.* 'Aureoreticulata', with gold-veined leaves, and even this is at its best in early summer; a vigorous and undemanding climber with small yellow flowers over a long season, very fragrant but not produced in great quantities at any one time.

*Passiflora caerulea* (passion flower): climbs by tendrils. Will often survive for many years in sheltered situations in southern England, in which case it remains semi-evergreen. If side growths are cut back to main branches in spring the plant will cover itself in elegant, lobed leaves and exquisitely formed flowers ringed with blue, white, green and black. After a hot summer golden-orange fruits are formed. It grows vigorously even in poor soils.

*Pileostegia viburnoides*: clings by aerial rootlets and, like most plants climbing naturally by aerial rootlets, it can also be woven through trellis for support. Not a spectacular climber, but its long, dark green leaves and panicles of feathery white flowers, produced in late summer, have a quiet distinction; grows well in most situations including shade.

In addition to the true climbers there are many evergreen shrubs which may be trained more or less closely against a wall or trellis. Some of the most vigorous and attractive are *Azara dentata* (yellow, strongly scented flowers), *Ceanothus impressus* (blue flowers in great abundance), *Solanum crispum* (blue/purple flowers throughout the summer) and *S. jasminoides* (blue or white flowers in late summer and autumn). All of these require a sunny position, the solanums being rather tender. *Garrya elliptica* (long green and cream catkins in winter) and *Pyracantha coccinea* (white flowers followed by red fruits), on the other hand, will grow in shaded positions, the former flowering moderately well even in heavy shade.

## Deciduous climbers

The choice of deciduous climbers is legion, so there is room here only to indicate a few of the most useful plants.

*Abutilon megapotamicum*: a slender wall shrub rather than a climber, needs to be tied back to its support. Although rather tender it is worth growing for the delightful turban flowers of red and yellow borne in endless succession through the year.

*Clematis*: cling by leaf petioles. Hybrids of the Jackmanii type are too well known to require description but are better as decoration than as screens, being slight in growth. More useful for screening is *Clematis tangutica*, with yellow lanterns over a long period of late summer followed by silver seedheads over an even longer season. *Clematis montana* 'Rubens' is also widely grown and very vigorous, but the white-flowered *C. montana* itself is surprisingly little known: a rather less vigorous plant with smaller and sweetly scented flowers which show up well in the shade in which it flourishes.

*Fallopia* (*Polygonum*) *baldschuanicum* (Russian vine, also aptly known as 'mile-a-minute'): climbs by twining stems. Almost legendary for its rapid growth. It is very undemanding and produces masses of white flowers, fading to pink, for many weeks in late summer. Its tremendous growth can be an asset or a liability depending on circumstances but the plant has little to recommend it when not in flower.

*Hydrangea petiolaris*: clings by aerial rootlets. Grows more slowly than the clematis and is altogether a more distinguished plant, with large, lace-cap inflorescences on warm reddish stems. It too, grows well in shade and its flowers are then even more lasting.

*Jasminum nudiflorum*: a stiff, ungainly shrub which may be tied back to resemble a climber; its toughness and abundance of yellow flowers in the depths of winter make it invaluable despite its overall lack of grace.

*Lonicera periclymenum*: climbs by twining stems. Our native honeysuckle, deservedly popular for its rich fragrance, especially as a combination of 'Early Dutch' and 'Late Dutch' varieties extend the flowering season. *Lonicera* × *tellmanniana* and *L. tragophylla* are unfortunately entirely without scent but are worth growing for their purple young foliage and large deep yellow flowers.

*Parthenocissus quinquefolia* (Virginia creeper): clings by aerial rootlets. An undemanding, vigorous grower with palmate leaves on long petioles. Autumn colour develops early and brilliantly in sun but it will colour fairly well even in shade.

*P. tricuspidata* (Boston ivy): has a closer habit and entire leaves. It clings more firmly to rough supports. On an open fence the Virginia creeper is preferable; Boston ivy is at its best clinging to a wall like a rich green tile-handing.

Roses: require tying to supports. They are valued for their flowers but have little else to recommend them as climbers, except perhaps 'Mermaid' with its semi-evergreen glossy foliage. Climbing roses have an open, stiff habit and tend to flower only at the top, but where space is not limited rambler roses may be used. Their laxer growth and vigorous, leafy habit look more natural on screens.

*Vitis* species: climb by tendrils. Make excellent screens in summer but are of little value in winter. *Vitis vinifera*, the grape vine, may be grown outside and in sheltered situations several modern cultivars will produce a good crop of grapes in most years. Other types are more used for ornament than for their small fruits, such as 'Brant' with rich autumn colour, and 'Purpurea', with purple leaves. Most spectacular of the vines is *V. coignetiae* with enormous leaves, which colour brilliantly in autumn.

*Wisteria sinensis* (Chinese wisteria): climbs by twining stems. Vigorous, but often slow to flower. A warm situation, restricted root-room and regular pruning back of long shoots will encourage flowering or plants can be grown in pots for a year or two, until root confinement forces flowering, then planted in the open ground. It can be used as a screen (sparse in winter), but is best overhead where the long racemes of flower can hang down.

## Climbers for temporary screening

These are all annuals or tender perennials and are best sown individually in small pots for planting outside when frost hazard is past. They require rich soil for rapid growth. Perennials may live for several years in mild situations.

*Cobaea scandens*: climbs by tendrils. Large purple/blue bell-shaped flowers. Perennial but seldom survives winter outside.

*Humulus japonicus* (annual hop): climbs by twining stems. Grown for attractive, light green palmate leaves; flowers green. Hardy annual.

*Ipomaea* 'Heavenly Blue' (morning glory): climbs by twining stems. Large, clear blue convolvulus-like flowers. Half-hardy annual for warm situation.

*Lathyrus odoratus* (sweet pea): climbs by tendrils. Very sweetly scented pea flowers in enormous range of colours. Hardy annual but may be sown in autumn/winter under cold glass for early plants. Tends to die out by midsummer in a dry season.

*Mutisia clematis*, *M. ilicifolia*, etc. (climbing gazania): climbs by tendrils. Little known but colourful climber with large daisy-like flowers in orange or pink/mauve. Perennial only in mildest situations and best grown as half-hardy annual in sheltered position.

*Passiflora caerulea* (passion flower): described above as a perennial evergreen climber (page 31). May be grown as an annual in less favoured climates.

*Pharbitis purpurea* (convolvulus): climbs by twining stems. Bright, funnel-shaped flowers in many shades of red/purple/blue/white. Hardy annual. Do not sow the dwarf bedding type by mistake!

*Phaseolus vulgaris* (runner bean): climbs by twining stems. This popular and very useful vegetable was first introduced as a flowering plant, and its decorative effect is being recognized anew with the pressing need to combine beauty and utility in small gardens. There are now pink- and white-flowered types as well as red. Perennial but usually grown as an annual.

*Tropaeolum canariensis* (canary creeper): climbs by twining stems. An elegant climber with fringed, yellow flowers. Like other tropaeolums – indeed like many other succulent climbers – it can be crippled by black fly. Hardy annual but best started under glass for rapid growth.

*Tropaeolum majus* (nasturtium): climbs by twining stems. Brilliant red, orange or yellow flowers, often sweetly scented but produced among pungent mustardy flavoured and edible leaves. Very susceptible to blackfly. Hardy annual.

### Shrubs for rapid screening

Most are too spreading in habit for permanent hedges except in large gardens but make excellent temporary windbreaks or vigorous 'fillers' where an 'instant' garden is required. Very few may be sheared satisfactorily.

*Berberis* × *stenophylla*: small, dark, evergreen leaves; scented orange flowers in early summer; arching, spreading and very prickly shrub making dense barrier. Can be sheared after flowering to make a compact hedge if required; not especially quick-growing but easily obtained and successfully moved as large plants.

*Buddleia alternifolia*: wide-spreading shrub with narrow grey-green leaves and small lavender flowers on arching branches; elegant and not to be confused with *B. davidii*. Clipping destroys form but spreading branches can be removed to encourage vertical growth.

*Cotoneaster* 'Cornubia': vigorous shrub with dark, glossy green leaves and large trusses of white flowers followed by red fruits. May be clipped but flowering and fruiting is then seriously impaired.

*Elaeagnus* × *ebbingei*: handsome, upright plant with dark evergreen glossy leaves, silver beneath. Makes excellent informal
hedge without shaping and is tolerant of salt; intolerant of
pruning.

*Escallonia* hybrids: larger, glossier-leaved types are fastest
growers, most nearly evergreen but least hardy; suitable
mainly for the south-west. 'Crimson Spire', 'C.F. Ball', 'Red
Guard' are especially good. 'Iveyi' is an excellent tall, late-
flowering white cultivar. Flower most freely when unpruned
but can be cut back very hard to encourage new growth
when they become too large; partially salt-tolerant.

*Ligustrum ovalifolium* (oval-leaf privet): more evergreen and
better-looking than *L. vulgare*. Quick-growing, very cheap
hedge but requires frequent shearing to maintain dense
hedge; salt-tolerant.

*Salix* species (willow): by inserting large, leafless cuttings in
winter and stooling hard, a cheap but not very dense hedge
can be obtained very quickly. Suitable only for wet situations. *S. alba* (white willow) is very fast and will make an
effective tall screen, rather open in winter; attractive greyish
foliage. *S. caprea* (goat willow) is fairly dense but undistinguished. *S. daphnoides* (violet willow) is extremely fast but
open; very decorative white stems. *S. elaeagnos* (hoary
willow) is fairly dense with attractive silver leaves; black
stems. Many willows can also be woven to form 'living
fences'.

*Sarothamnus scoparius* (broom): fast-growing but short-lived
and rather open plant; long season of scented yellow
flowers. Can be sheared lightly after flowering to encourage
more compact habit but best as temporary screen on light
soils; use small, pot-grown plants.

## Shrubs for visual softening

The following are again quick-growing plants but are unsuitable for windbreaks, being too thin or too tender. However

they are excellent tall plants for breaking the outlines of fences, sheds and similar features. Several are quite tender and must be sited with considerable care.

*Abutilon vitifolium*: will grow 2m (6ft) in a year and 3m (10ft) in two years with no trouble; it will then grow only slowly in height but spreads into a more shapely form. Flowers, mauve or white, are produced over a long season to complement the greyish foliage. Although not completely hardy it can be propagated easily from cuttings to safeguard against loss.

*Buddleia davidii* and *B. fallowiana*: gaunt shrubs but grow up quickly and have attractive flowers. The latter has grey foliage, scented lavender flowers and more substance. *B. alternifolia* is also useful (see list of rapid screening shrubs above).

*Ceanothus impressus*: has small, dark, crinkled evergreen leaves and is smothered in rich blue flowers in early summer. Although somewhat tender and usually grown as a wall shrub it makes a tall mound if grown in the open, and flowers even more freely until killed by a hard winter.

*Cytisus battandieri*: has elegant silky grey foliage and clusters of rich yellow scented flowers in June, an excellent companion for the ceanothus. Also tender, especially as a young plant.

*Fremontodendron (Fremontia) californicum*: its dark green leaves, felted white beneath, and yellow flowers are very attractive. The most tender plant in this list but grows very rapidly so is easily, and fairly inexpensively, replaced if disaster befalls it.

*Genista aetnensis* (Mount Etna broom): light, airy growth with sweetly scented yellow flowers in late summer. Although taking three to four years to grow appreciably, it will then assume the form of an elegant small tree and will enhance the garden for many years, especially on light soil.

## Shrubs for exposed situations

Although not growing as quickly as the hedges listed above, the following make excellent, usually permanent hedges for coastal or upland areas.

*Caragana arborescens*: fairly fast-growing and upright shrub which tolerates very low temperatures and strong winds; glaucous foliage and sparse yellow pea-like flowers.

*Crataegus oxyacantha* (hawthorn): dense, thorny and hardy shrub or small tree; moderately fast although will obviously grow more slowly in hostile situation; very cheap to buy.

*Hippophäe rhamnoides* (sea buckthorn): extremely tough shrub for severely exposed situations; not very dense or shapely but has attractive silver leaves and orange fruits; intolerant of shade.

*Ilex aquifolium* (holly): an excellent, dense hedge tolerant of salt, exposure and a wide range of soil conditions; slow growing, rather expensive to buy and the spiky fallen leaves can be a nuisance.

*Olearia* species: for mild areas only; rather slow growing but making dense, compact hedges with dark, leathery leaves very resistant to salt and wind damage. *Olearia* × *haastii* and *O. macrodonta* are commonly used but there are several other attractive, more tender – and more expensive – species.

*Prunus lusitanica* (Portugal laurel): not for the most exposed areas but a tall, evergreen hedge suitable for most soils, in shade and in relatively cold, windy areas; a much better and hardier plant for hedging than the common laurel.

*Prunus spinosa* (blackthorn): stiffly upright, suckering plant; not suitable for small gardens but very hardy.

*Quercus ilex* (evergreen or holm oak): slow to establish but eventually makes a good, dense hedge; slightly damaged by salt or extreme cold and best on well-drained soil.

*Rhamnus cathartica* (common buckthorn) and *R. frangula*

(alder buckthorn): vigorous, upright shrubs suitable for exposed situations, on dry, chalky soils and wet, peaty soils respectively.

*Rosa rugosa*: a delightful garden shrub with magenta, pink or white flowers, large red heps and yellow foliage in autumn; it is also a very tough, suckering and vigorous plant suitable for making low windbreaks on most soils, but expecially on sandy soils.

*Sambucus nigra* (common elder): not suitable for small, tidy hedges but a vigorous, hardy plant for inclusion in pioneer windbreaks.

*Senecio greyi et al.*: the shrubby senecios are suitable only for low hedges, eventually up to 1.5m (5ft), but are very wind- and salt-tolerant and surprisingly good in shade; also good for planting on banks or dry walls to increase the height of shelter; grey foliage (dark green with felty white reverse in *S. monroi*) and yellow daisy flowers.

## COPING WITH SHADE

Solutions to the problems of over-exposure to wind or sun have been considered in the earlier part of this chapter. Under-exposure is a problem which often just has to be lived with.

### Shade from buildings

Shade from buildings is definite and predictable. In Britain, shade on the north side of a building extends for half of the building's height at midday in summer and five times its height in midwinter. Direct sunlight falls only before 6am and after 6pm GMT in summer and not at all in winter. West-facing walls cast very long shadows in the morning (incidentally safe-guarding tender plants from thawing too rapidly after frost), but the shadow quickly shortens to disappear by midday. In the afternoon and evening, when the sun is at its strongest, a west-facing wall is entirely unshaded. For east-facing walls the picture is reversed, with shadows lengthening rapidly in the afternoon. South-facing walls receive maximum radiation and are free of shadows for most of the day. They are, however, shaded in early morning and in the evening during the summer, a point worth remembering when planning for the use of the garden during long summer evenings: a north or, ideally, north-west facing wall receives the last of the summer evening sunshine.

## Shade from trees

Shade from trees is less complete and less predictable as trees grow in size and usually shed their leaves in winter. Tree shade can also be modified by careful thinning and pruning. However, once a tree is severely pruned the balance between roots and branches is upset and regular shaping will be required thereafter to redress the balance. Also, even drastic thinning of the crown will not materially affect dryness caused by tree roots, the other problem associated with gardening in the shade. The pruning of trees is dealt with in some detail in Chapter 4, but it is important to emphasize here that reshaping should be undertaken with the greatest caution. Trees add so much to the character of a garden that one should work with them rather than against them whenever possible.

It must also be emphasized that shade is by no means entirely undesirable. It is frequently pleasant to escape to a shaded corner in summer even in Britain; shade adds privacy and an atmosphere of mystery in small gardens; it highlights plants growing in sunlight nearby and there is a wide range of interesting plants which can be grown in shade to create cool, refreshing gardens of great charm.

When shade is excessive, however, tackling of the problem can be considered in three stages: planning to make maximum use of sunlight; techniques to bring additional light into the garden; treatment of the remaining, heavily shaded areas.

## Planning a shaded garden

### Large gardens

Large gardens are seldom entirely shaded and most of the shade will be from trees. Sunny corners near the house can be earmarked for sitting areas, pools – both ornamental and swimming – and other features requiring illumination. Larger open areas will be used for fruit, vegetables and lawns, all of which require high light intensities for satisfactory growth. This will leave the shaded parts of the garden for ornamental plants capable of tolerating such situations. If there is insufficient room in the open for lawn and kitchen garden, priorities will have to be considered. One thinks automatically of a lawn as an essential for children to play on and of vegetables as being ugly, to be banished from the immediate vicinity of the house – but neither of these assumptions is an absolute truth.

A paved terrace and the garden paths offer excellent playgrounds for children when the ground is wet underfoot, especially if a covered sandpit is incorporated in the terrace (perhaps to be made into a lily pool subsequently) and the paths offer a complete circuit for tricycles and scooters. For summer weather the tree-shaded area can be put to use. The best site for a 'woodland playground' is usually obvious: some clearing among the trees is desirable; a tree or trees with many low branches for climbing and a strong high branch for ladders, swings or trapeze are valuable assets, but if the 'woodland' is merely a patch of sycamore seedlings and scrubby small trees there is still scope for careful thinning and there can be a climbing frame, swings and log cabin even if all the timber is imported.

Overthinning should be avoided as weedy sycamores and scruffy bamboos will create secrecy, adventure and, at the right age of the children, an endless supply of spears, arrows, oars and other vital equipment. If the 'woodland' is a real woodland, well endowed with tall trees but too open beneath, a planting of hazel, bamboo or other cover while children are toddlers will prove a wise investment as both plants and children grow. An even wiser investment is to teach children from an early age to respect territorial rights and to use tools safely.

Paved areas and woodland having been designated for recreation and enjoyment, the small and precious open area near the house could then be devoted to vegetables grown in a formal and attractive garden. Examples of ornamental vegetable gardens are now becoming quite frequent as lack of space forces the kitchen garden into public gaze. With a simple pattern of paths, arches for runner beans, perhaps wires for espalier fruits and beds of vegetables edged with parsley or thyme, lavender or box, an erstwhile mundane necessity can be turned into a major decorative feature.

## Small gardens

In small gardens, the problems of shade can be more serious with no opportunity to escape from the north wall of the house to a distant patch of sunshine. Walled town gardens, perhaps with a large plane or sycamore near by, may have sunshine for only a few hours each day in midsummer and none at all from September to March. In such cases any thoughts of a traditional lawn should be abandoned. Grass does not grow well in shade. It will not tolerate hard wear and the cutting of a tiny patch of lawn presents problems: it is too small to warrant a lawn mower and too tedious to cut by hand. The presence of a thin, patchy, damp, mossy, yellow-green lawn emphasizes the gloom of a garden rather than relieving it. It is better, therefore, to decide which is the sunniest (or rather the least shady) part of the garden and to pave it attractively.

With sunlight at a premium, there are two possible approaches to the design of the garden: to bring as much light as possible into the garden or to use the shade to create a woodland garden in miniature.

## Bringing light into a shaded garden

### Walls and paving

Light colours and reflective surfaces can do much to brighten a dull garden. Walls provide the largest surface in town gardens and painting the walls white is a good start. A white floor may seem the next step but this is as sensible as a white carpet in the playroom. White concrete discolours to a dingy grey if walked on and will show every footmark as well as greening over if damp. A light stone colour is eminently more satisfactory: York stone might have been invented for the purpose but artificial stone is available in a range of pale buffs and greys. It is cheaper, rather more in keeping with a bright white surround and not slippery when wet. Real stone in damp, shady situations is highly dangerous to walk on!

### Water in shaded gardens

Pools will also reflect light. The pool should be small in relation to the size of garden: as it must occupy a sunny position to be effective, it competes directly with the area devoted to paving. Suitably sited, a raised pool will catch the sun before light reaches the paving, bringing precious extra minutes of sunshine, and if the pool has a fountain this will sparkle with sunlight even earlier in the day. In small shaded gardens water is required for its reflective quality, so the surface should not be smothered or hemmed in by too much planting. It may be treated entirely artificially, kept clean and sparkling by chemicals, or partly artificially with perhaps one small water-lily and a slender grassy clump to emphasize the 'wateriness' of the pond and a few goldfish. Too complicated an attempt to introduce marginal plants and other complexities in a small and often shaded pool is inviting disaster in the form of a green smelly mess.

*Mirrors in the shaded garden*

Mirrors can be even more useful than pools, both reflecting light into the garden and reflecting images to give a greater sense of spaciousness. In theory the use of mirrors sounds gimmicky but in reality they can be most effective. Careful placing is required, however. Reflected light should illuminate the garden, not dazzle the observer, and the mirror should reflect attractive aspects of the garden, again *not* the observer. It is most disconcerting to sit in or wander round a garden and be constantly confronted with oneself! Mirrors at the end of a pergola to give an impression of added length can be particularly unnerving in this respect.

For these reasons it is wise to experiment with the placing of a large mirror before settling on a permanent position. When the position has been decided the mirror should be mounted securely and its edges obscured by trailing plants. The effect should be of a window of light opening from the garden, not a piece of bedroom furniture left outside by mistake.

*Contrast in the shaded garden*

White walls, light paving, pools and mirrors can improve the appearance of a dark garden immensely, but these ideas should not be carried too far. Too much white results in a hard, clinical, boxed-in atmosphere, the very antithesis of a relaxing garden, and unrelieved whiteness without direct illumination will pall to dingy grey. Contrast is needed before the whiteness can be fully appreciated. A black tracery on the walls, whether of simple trellis, wrought-iron scrollwork or dark-leaved climber will throw the wall into sharp relief and make it sparkle even without direct sunlight.

A small walled garden may be shaded but it will also be sheltered: the white walls, water, and mirrors will create an ideal background for bold foliage plants whether tender – canna, caladium, nelumbo or even bananas in large tubs – or the hardier fatsia, mahonia, catalpa and acanthus. Dark, bold foliage against white walls is particularly amenable to artificial lighting in the evening to create striking effects and extend the usefulness of the garden. The plants will create black shadows against which the general shade of the garden appears light by contrast.

The shadows and dark leaves serve in turn as a background for white furniture, sculpture or small flowers: snowdrops and *Anemone nemorosa* early in the year, small hostas later on and the amazingly resilient *Cyclamen hederifolium (neapolitanum)* 'Album' in the autumn. To this short list of perennials may also be added white *Begonia semperflorens*, perfumed tobacco plants and white 'geraniums' (zonal pelargoniums). Thus a white box with a rim of dark plants becomes diversified into a mosaic of dark and light, with the emphasis on light.

### Colour in the shaded garden
Against this monochrome effect, colour is best used in strong, concentrated spots: a tub of scarlet 'geraniums', crimson begonia or orange dahlias, or groups of coloured-leaved plants. Yellow flowers are on the whole best avoided, unless they are a bright orange-yellow. Lemony yellows fade to green in poor light and are not conspicuous.

Choice of plants plays a vital role in developing a shady garden, more so than in any other circumstances, and this is especially so when the other approach mentioned above – the creation of a miniature 'woodland garden' – is adopted.

## Planting for a woodland effect
When a garden is already heavily shaded by buildings, tree planting can do little additional harm and much good. The tree canopy catches the sun even when the garden itself is in shade, and the sparkling effect of sunlit foliage is pleasant whether viewed from below, in the garden, or above, from the upper windows of the house. When a miniature 'woodland' character is created, the shade becomes more attractive, more acceptable

than the solid grey gloom cast by buildings. Furthermore, if spotlighting is used in the garden, lighting of trees from below gives an enchanting effect of being in a soft green cave.

## Trees for the shaded garden

Trees must, of course, be chosen with great care. Light foliage is useful but silver-leaved pear, whitebeam and other grey-leaved trees are too solid for a small garden and too sombre if not illuminated directly by sunlight. *Prunus subhirtella* has light, open and attractively glossy foliage and the form *P.s.* 'Autumnalis' produces dainty pink flowers throughout the winter months. This graceful cherry is not to be confused with the Japanese cherries with their heavy form and foliage. Birches, too, are graceful and light, especially the Swedish or cut-leaved birch, *Betula pendula* 'Dalecarlica'. The weeping *B.p.* 'Youngii' is also very beautiful if it is trained to a good height before being allowed to cascade, otherwise it slouches about and fills a small garden with unwanted twiggery. Purple-leaved birch is dramatic but not very conspicuous in shade, while the yellow-leaved *B. pubescens* 'Aurea' is of good colouring but very rare, very slow-growing and *very* expensive. Yellow and yellow-green foliage in general is good at simulating a 'sunshine streaming through beechwoods in spring' quality in the garden and there are two outstanding trees of this colouring, *Gleditsia triacanthos* 'Sunburst' and *Robinia pseudoacacia* 'Frisia'. The former, a brilliant acid yellow fading eventually to green, is slower in growth, more sparse in branching and the better choice for restricted space. The latter is a soft, warmer yellow which fades only a little. Its growth, too, is softer, fuller and faster but it will stay within bounds for many years. As mentioned earlier, both have the endearing habit of coming into leaf later than most trees and gleditsia loses its leaves early in the autumn, so their canopies of shade are there only when most needed.

All these trees will eventually become fairly large, some quite quickly, but this should not preclude their use in small gardens: just the opposite. Limiting planting to small plants merely emphasizes the cramped meanness of a garden. True, one may be able to cultivate five thousand alpines or dwarfs in the space taken by five trees, but the impression given is of a crowded and cramped yard. Where the garden is more important than the plants, five trees are the better bet, perhaps with five hundred woodland carpeters beneath as a charming compromise! Young trees are very easily pruned to keep them within bounds and even if this is too much trouble, they will not outgrow their situation for at least ten years. £25–£30 for ten years of increasing pleasure must surely be the best bargain of the twenty-first century.

## Planting beneath trees

Planting below trees also allows much scope. Many dark-leaved evergreens not only tolerate shade, but look more elegantly dark and glossy than in sunnier situations. *Prunus lusitanica, Ligustrum lucidum, Viburnum tinus, Viburnum davidii, Sarcococca ruscifolia, Liriope muscari, Helleborus foetidus* and *Asarum europaeum* are but a few, from the very large to the very small, whose dark glossiness emphasizes the blackness of shade and act as an ideal foil for pale flowers and lighter foliage displayed against them.

### *White flowers for the shaded garden*

Perhaps it is not a coincidence that most of the plants mentioned in the preceding paragraph have white flowers; certainly, white shows up beautifully in shaded situations. Fortunately, there are many other white flowers which tolerate shade.

Snowdrops, crocus (spring and autumn) and *Anemone nemorosa* will flourish in shade. Narcissus tends to produce more leaf than flower and tulips require regular renewal, but neither are expensive and even small groups are very effective. *Sanguinaria canadensis* requires a moist, leafy soil but must be counted among the most beautiful of woodland plants. The same remarks apply to the later-flowering *Trillium grandiflorum* and exotic *Arisaema candidissima*. All have elegant foliage in addition to exquisite flowers. Lily of the valley and Solomon's seal are tougher but no less desirable. The variegated forms of both add interest after flowering. *Iris sibirica* 'White Swirl' glistens in shade, as do *Hosta plantaginea* (*subcordata*) and the white forms of Japanese anemone later in the season. All three, rather surprisingly, tolerate fairly dry situations although they are much finer in moist soils. White forget-me-nots and foxgloves will seed themselves freely and can be thinned to create naturalistic colonies with very little effort.

*Yellow-leaved and variegated plants for the shaded garden*
Many yellow-leaved and variegated plants are at their best in shade: not only are the colours best appreciated there, but they escape the scorching which is a problem in full sun.

Among the yellow plants, creeping jenny (*Lysimachia nummularia* 'Aurea'), yellow ivies such as 'Buttercup' and 'Gold Heart', *Filipendula ulmaria* 'Aurea', *Ribes sanguineun* 'Brocklebankii', *Weigela* 'Looymansii Aurea', golden elder and golden privet offer a range of forms and beautiful foliage textures for shade.

The variegated forms of *Brunnera macrophylla*, *Acorus calamus*, *Iris foetidissima* and the Solomon's seal already mentioned above have conspicuous white markings as do several of the hostas. Although the markings are more pronounced in full sun, the leaves expand more fully in shade and the markings are protected from shrivelling to an unpleasant brown.

These clean white stripes do not always associate well with the acid yellow leaves of the first group, but *Cornus alba* 'Elegantissima' (white variegated), *C.a.* 'Spaethii' (yellow variegated), ivies, *Persicaria virginiana* 'Painter's Palette' and variegated lily of the valley are sufficiently variable and creamy in their colouring to provide colour gradations between the two extremes.

## Other foliage plants

Shade also encourages the expansion of many other beautiful leaves. Several foliage plants have already been mentioned in other contexts, but one could add to the list at least *Aruncus dioicus*, *Paeonia mlokosewitschii*, *Tiarella cordifolia*, the epimediums and the enormous family of ferns. As many of these tolerate not only shade, but dry shade too, they are discussed more fully below.

### COPING WITH DRY SHADE

If shade is cast by large trees rather than by buildings, the scope for additional planting is very much reduced because trees will extract water and nutrients from the soil but an attractive garden is still possible. In some instances the root problem can be overcome temporarily by digging a trench to sever invading roots but this is seldom advisable. Such root-pruning can endanger the stability and even the life of a tree, putting surrounding properties at risk and new roots soon colonize as vigorously as before. One can – and should – improve the soil by digging in and mulching with organic material, adding fertilizers and irrigating in dry periods, but the best long-term solution is to use tough, reliable perennial plants.

Much disappointment is caused by a common misunderstanding so it must be emphasized here that no plant will luxuriate in a rootfilled, shaded soil under a dense, leafy tree. Plants listed as tolerant of such situations will indeed tolerate, but they will not flourish. For this reason, annuals are a complete loss. Starved, shaded and droughtstricken annuals will struggle to produce a few flowers before winter sets in. Perennial plants are required, for these can increase slowly but steadily over the years to furnish the garden. Growth can be increased enormously by generous feeding and watering in the first year or two before leaving the plants to fend for themselves, and careful choice and generous planting can soon create an excellent, mature effect.

## Plants for dry shade

*Viburnum tinus* and privet occupy many a dusty shrubbery but the viburnum is almost unrecognizable in the glossy elegance it assumes in shade and the large-leaved, large-flowered *Ligustrum lucidum* is a distinguished plant in any setting. Neither will flower as abundantly in shade as in the open – no plant will – but the inflorescences are larger and laxer to compensate in part. *Lonicera pileata* looks rather like a diminutive, horizontal privet. It is not quite evergreen but this is an advantage as the new foliage, very early in the year, is a bright, fresh and cheerful spring green. *Choisya ternata* is evergreen. It is also slightly tender but is less likely to be damaged by frost in shade, which it tolerates extremely well. *Sarcococca*, the compact *Euphorbia characias* (*wulfenii*) and the rampageous *E. robbiae* are evergreen at a lower level as are the enormously varied ivies not forgetting the arborescent, non-trailing forms which make attractively rounded shrubs. My favourite ivy is *Hedera helix* 'Erecta' which grows in a slightly bizarre, stiffly erect fashion as if imitating an Irish yew. Hollies, both green and variegated are so amenable to pruning that they can assume any proportions from low ground-cover to tall trees.

Of the ground-covers proper, three are particularly noteworthy: lamium, pachysandra and vinca. *Lamium maculatum* would be useful for its leaves alone, dark green with a brilliant white central zone, but it also has attractive flowers, a hard magenta-pink in the species but clear pink or white in the forms *L.m.* 'Roseum' and 'Album'. *L.m.* 'Album' is especially vigorous without being invasive. *L. galeobdolon* 'Variegatum' on the other hand is very invasive, not underground fortunately, but it throws long trailing shoots up into shrubs, eventually smothering all but the tallest of them. It should only be grown among trees with clear, unbranched trunks, in which situation it is extremely handsome, far more attractive than in the open, when it becomes a pallid yellow. *L.g.* 'Silberteppich' (silver carpet) is much more compact and has elegantly silvered foliage. Although very different in habit, *Pachysandra terminalis* shares the characteristic of paling unpleasantly in full sun. In shade, even in deep shade, its fresh green rosettes spread by underground rhizomes (slowly at first) to make a neat, even carpet. Its flowers are small and green, interesting but not exciting. *Vinca major* and its brightly cream-variegated form share the looping growth of *Lamium galeobdolon* at a less frightening and more manageable pace and their looseness makes them suitable only for large areas. They are visually too thin for small patches to be effective. *Vinca minor*, however, is small, neat and very robust, vigorous and attractive enough to use for large expanses but neat enough to be used in small gardens among other plants. There are variegated forms as well as variants in flower colour.

*Mahonia aquifolium* is a much-maligned plant. It grows well in dry, shady situations, even beneath beech trees, but its old foliage is as drab and careworn in appearance as the young foliage is glossy, translucent and bronzed. Since, in heavy shade, it grows upward and slowly, old foliage outweighs the new, so this is a plant which looks infinitely more attractive if hard pruned at regular intervals after it is well established.

The bold-leaved *Fatsia japonica* and its trailing relation × *Fatshedera lizei* are often seen as house plants but are quite hardy in the south of Britain, and even more so in shade than in full sun.

However, too many evergreens – even with a fair sprinkling of variegated leaves or bold foliage such as *Fatsia* – can be depressingly solid. Some softer foliage is necessary for relief. Ferns are the epitome of soft foliage and several ferns will tolerate dry situations. Male fern, *Dryopteris filix-mas*, is best known in this respect, but polypody (*Polypodium vulgare*) and hartstongue (*Phyllitis scolopendrium*) are equally valuable. There are many attractively dissected forms of polypody and its close relative *Polypodium cambricum*. Disconcertingly the mature fronds brown and die in midsummer but are soon replaced by new growth which remains fresh and green throughout the winter months. *Polystichum setiferum* is a finer, softer fern which grows slowly but surely to form a large flat rosette of great delicacy. Like all the others its growth with abundant moisture is much superior in elegance and size but, without neighbouring super-plants to compare with, the results in dry shade leave little to be desired. To continue the theme of woodland grace established by the ferns one might add Solomon's seal (less menacingly invasive in dry soil), the perennial pale yellow foxglove *Digitalis grandiflora* (*ambigua*) and the many beautiful epimediums (which definitely tolerate rather than flourish in dry conditions). *Alchemilla mollis* is another low plant with many attributes. Much loved by flower arrangers, its rosettes of silky, yellow-green leaves are just the right colour to enhance the woodland character of a small garden. Its foaming flower heads are yellower than the leaves but not greatly so, and it is one of the very few plants which almost flourishes in dry shade. Indeed it is wise, when growing alchemilla in association with other plants, to shear off its flowers as soon as they fade to prevent the hordes of seedlings swamping less vigorous neighbours.

*Aruncus dioicus* will tower over all these plants with its divided foliage and creamy plumes of flower looking very much like a giant astilbe. The hellebores, especially *Helleborus foetidus*, and the fragile-looking but resilient *Paeonia mlokosewitschii* offer fine foliage and flowers at a lower level, while *Iris foetidissima*, especially in its variegated form, is an excellent sword-like foil. Two geraniums are among the most tolerant plants for really dry shade. *Geranium macrorrhizum* is the tidier but the looser, lighter and more slender *G. nodosum* is more attractive perhaps.

Lastly, at the bottom of the scale, are three 'bulbs' and two very different carpeting plants. *Anemone blanda*, *Cyclamen hederifolium* (*neapolitanum*) and the winter aconite *Eranthis hyemalis* are all sold by bulb merchants, although the second and third are much better if obtained as growing plants and watered in to the new situation. The cyclamen flowers in autumn, then produces marbled leaves which last to midsummer, whereas the anemone and the aconite, flowering very early in spring, then die away quickly. A carpet for them is therefore very desirable. *Viola riviana* 'Purpurea' (*V. labradorica*) is a violet with dark purple leaves and a habit of seeding freely. It can become a nuisance but a very nice one. *Asarina procumbens* (*Antirrhinum asarina*) is a looser but still ground-hugging carpet of grey woolly foliage on which yellow 'snapdragons' are borne in pairs for most of the late summer and autumn. Although a native of sun-baked Spanish hillsides, it makes an effective carpet beneath trees – even cedar trees – and seems undeterred by the dustiest of soils.

This is not a complete list of plants, of course. Many others could be mentioned, but the aim has been to present a few brief descriptions of highly desirable plants rather than a long list of meaningless names, and to demonstrate that a dry, shady garden need not be devoid of interest.

## KITCHEN GARDENING IN THE SHADE: VEGETABLES, FRUITS AND HERBS

The greatest difficulty of a shaded garden arises when the decision is made to produce home-grown fruit and vegetables. Fruits depend on flower production and on the accumulation of sugars in the plant, neither of which is favoured by low light intensity. Vegetables are almost invariably grown as annuals, sown and harvested within a year, and rapid growth is essential for first class results.

Acceptable results can, however, be produced by good cultivation if it is remembered that plants growing in shade will be taller, looser, leafier and lower in sugar than similar plants in a sunny situation. Shade stimulates leaf growth at the expense of roots, flower and fruits. Fertilizers with high phosphate and potash contents will stimulate sugar production, thus compensating in part for poor light conditions, whereas nitrogenous fertilizers will exacerbate the problem of low light.

Leafy crops such as leeks, lettuce, cabbages and even asparagus will grow quite well in partial shade, but hearting is affected by light intensity so non-hearting lettuce is more satisfactory, and rock-hard heads of cabbage should not be expected. Rhubarb is another leafy plant which tolerates shade, although its flavour is impaired in heavy shade.

Less satisfactory are root crops such as carrots, parsnips and beet. In shade, these produce abundant foliage but not much root, although heavy applications of potash especially will help to redress the balance. Least satisfactory are fruiting plants in general, whether consumed as fruits, (apples, peaches, figs) or as vegetables (tomatoes, peas, beans). Marrows, cucumbers and melon require high temperature rather than high light intensity for successful growth, so good crops can be had in shade especially if frames or cloches are used. Tomatoes, on the other hand, flower poorly and the fruits ripen slowly in shade. When the garden itself is not at all sunny it is advisable to devote a sunny window sill indoors to tomatoes: two or three plants will produce appreciable quantities of fruit.

Of the dessert fruits, alpine strawberries, raspberries and blackberries are found naturally in open woodland and will fruit in shade (although never so freely and sweetly as in a moist, sunny situation). Blackcurrants are less suitable, while large-fruited strawberries, like the tomato, are best regarded as decorative window-plants if the garden is unduly shaded. Plums and Morello cherries are traditionally associated with north-facing walls and will crop satisfactorily, whereas apples and pears, which ripen rather late in the year, and peaches and figs, which require ripening of the wood as well as of the fruit, are best avoided.

All this assumes that the shade comes from nearby buildings and that the garden is, as a result, shady and moist. If the shade is cast by trees which impoverish the soil by their massive root systems, then the effort required to cultivate, irrigate and feed crops will be out of all proportion to the results, unless of course (as is often the situation), the toil is considered a labour of love by the masochistic garden owner.

Herbs present a different proposition because although one associates most herbs with dry, sun-baked slopes, many are surprisingly tolerant of other conditions. Mint and parsley flourish in moist, shady situations. Chives and rosemary are also quite successful, as is Welsh onion, a useful perennial, clump-forming onion which can be grown where large onions would fail. Most of the grey-leaved herbs can be grown in similar situations for culinary use although they lose their colouring and compact habit and require frequent cutting back to keep them from looking bedraggled.

In dry shade the looseness of habit is not a problem. The perennial nature and adaptation to drought of many herbs mean that they will grow slowly but surely in the shade of trees. Lavender, sage and the taller thymes will all grow in such situations although they will not be at their best: lavender in particular often looks dingy in shade. Rosemary, however, is such a satisfying, healthy, dark green that it is worth noting for shady situations, wet or dry, whether or not it is required for culinary use.

One great joy of all the herbs is that they are quickly and easily propagated by cuttings or division, so it is possible to experiment with them in various situations at little or no expense.

# 2. Soil

There are two possible approaches to gardening on 'difficult' soils: choosing plants to suit the particular soil conditions or modifying the soil to suit particular plants. When growing ornamental plants, the former approach is far easier, cheaper and more satisfactory. With an enormous range of plants to choose from, it is not difficult to prepare a long list of those suitable for a particular soil type whereas soil modification has many pitfalls. Even if one succeeds in making chalk soils more acid, for example, they will still be excessively drained and situated in a dry part of the country, unsuitable for rhododendrons and their allies. It is better, therefore, to choose plants wisely and thus to create a flourishing garden stamped with local character rather than a pretentious failure.

The situation with culinary plants is rather different. The choice of fruits and vegetables is more limited and many belong to a few plant families having well-defined soil preferences. *Leguminosae* and *Cruciferae* are predominant among vegetables, while *Rosaceae* includes nearly all fruit crops. As most fruits and vegetables require a fertile soil and will tolerate quite a high degree of alkalinity, it is easier to alter the soil to suit the crops than to find fruits and vegetables which will tolerate difficult soils, although the latter is possible.

Soil treatment for lawns is more complex and is dealt with in Chapter 5.

## GENERAL PROPERTIES

It will be helpful to consider the properties of soils in general before discussing the improvement of particular types of soil.

## Soil texture

The bulk of soil is made up of mineral fragments resulting from the weathering of various rocks. If the fragments or particles were formed *in situ*, they will be of varied sizes and shapes. If they were carried by wind or water they will often be very uniform in shape and size and arranged in definite layers. The proportions of various sizes of particles in a soil, the soil texture, greatly influence its character.

### Gravel and sand

Gravel and sand are large particles which, when packed together, leave large gaps, or pores, between them. Water runs through these large pores very rapidly, washing away any nutrients and creating acid conditions. Soils with a high proportion of gravel or sand are therefore freely drained, they warm up quickly and can be cultivated early in the spring but they dry out badly in summer, are very poor in nutrients and usually very acid.

### Silt

Silt is finer than the finest sand. The particles are so fine that they pack tightly together when wet to form a hard crust. When dry and loose the silt particles blow about creating dust storms. Because of these problems true silt soils are very difficult to cultivate unless organic matter is present in large quantities. Most so-called 'silt soils' are in fact mixtures of fine sand and clay deposited at river mouths. They are very fertile and less difficult to manage than true silts.

### Clay

Clay particles are even smaller and have quite different properties from those of sand and silt. They have a layered structure with plant nutrients sandwiched between the layers. Because of their chemical structure they are negatively charged and therefore attract positively charged molecules including potassium, magnesium, iron and calcium, all important plant nutrients. Soils with high clay contents are therefore usually rich in nutrients and the nutrients are not easily washed out of the soil but, because of the very small particle size, and hence very fine pores between them, water moves very slowly. Clay soils drain only slowly: they are slow to warm up in spring but retain water for use by plants into the summer, by which time sandy soils are very dry. They may also swell and shrink dramatically as they wet and dry, causing wide cracks to appear in dry summers.

Mixtures of sand, silt and clay have the advantages of all their constituents. Nutrients and water are retained by the clay while the sand makes the soil more open, more workable and more easily drained of excess water. Well-balanced mixtures of sand, silt and clay are called 'loam', while soils with a preponderance of one or other particle type may be sandy loams, clay loams, etc.

## Soil structure

The texture of a soil is obviously very important in affecting its fertility but soil structure is equally important. The various soil particles are bound together by clay or sticky organic gums produced by bacteria etc., to form soil-crumbs. Decay of roots, activity of worms, swelling and shrinking of clay as it wets and dries all create larger cracks and pores, so a well-structured soil will have a wide range of pore sizes from worm-holes and root channels, which drain rapidly and aerate the soil, to very fine pores, which retain water for use by plants during dry periods.

Unlike texture, which is more or less constant, soil structure is very much affected by cultivation. Working the soil when it is wet is very harmful as any pressure on the soil-water is transmitted through the soil, shattering crumbs, puddling the soil and altering the arrangement of the particles so they set to a hard, concrete-like mass. Freezing has the opposite effect:

enlarging ice crystals withdraw water from the soil mass and press the drying soil into tight crumbs. As the soil thaws, the crumbs can separate and a once sticky lump of clay will fall apart into a crumbly soil with the slightest knock of a rake or fork.

## Organic matter

Organic matter, although seldom forming more than five per cent of the soil, has an importance out of all proportion to its presence. The breakdown of organic material releases nutrients in forms easily taken up and used by plants. The micro-organisms causing the breakdown also produce sticky secretions which help to cement soil particles into a stable structure. The partially decayed organic material, or humus, also acts as a sponge, holding enormous quantities of water (many times its own weight) for use by plant roots. Addition of organic material, whether manure, compost, peat, spent hops, straw or paper shreds, etc., will improve any soil, although most materials (except manure and compost) will actually remove nitrogen from the soil while they are decomposing, so it is wise to add a generous application of nitrogenous fertilizer when digging in such materials. The one situation in which it is unwise to add organic material is when the soil is likely to become waterlogged. The breakdown of organic matter in waterlogged conditions produces compounds which can kill plant roots.

## Soil pH

Acidity and alkalinity are measured on a pH scale from 0 (very acid) to 14 (very alkaline). pH 7 is neutral and in soil the range rarely extends below pH 3.5 for the most acid peat bogs, or above pH 8.5 for very alkaline chalk soils and salt marshes.

The pH of a soil is very important as it is a vital factor in determining which plants will and will not survive. Plants vary a great deal in their tolerance of acid or alkaline soil. A few – of minor importance in gardens – will only grow in strongly alkaline soils. A great many more will grow only on acid soils, while the majority will grow in any soil that is neither extremely acid nor extremely alkaline. Even this tolerant majority, however, will usually grow more satisfactorily on one side of neutral than the other.

In very acid soils, nitrogen is usually lacking, phosphate may be leached (washed out of the soil as rain drains through it) and minerals such as manganese and aluminium become available in the soil in quantities which are harmful or even fatal to most plants.

In very alkaline soils, phosphate, magnesium and iron become unavailable. They are still present in the soil but in forms that plants cannot readily use. As magnesium and iron are required by all green plants for the making of chlorophyll – the green material essential to plant life – plants unable to obtain these minerals in alkaline conditions become very pale yellow-green, or 'chlorotic'.

Although pH is determined naturally by the soil type it can be altered by chemical treatment. Such treatment, whether liming to increase pH or acidification to reduce it, is an essential part of the management of soil fertility and is discussed in the following sections dealing with particularly difficult soils.

## Plant nutrients

In addition to providing anchorage and a water supply for plants the soil is the main source of plant nutrients, the most important of which are nitrogen, phosphorus, potassium, magnesium, iron and calcium, with another dozen or so required in much smaller quantities.

### Nitrogen

Nitrogen is used to make protein in the plant. It exists in the soil as nitrate which is not held on clay particles and is therefore easily leached (washed out of the topsoil by rainfall), so regular addition is required. Organic nitrogen compounds release nitrogen gradually, regulating its supply and preventing its leaching. Ammonium compounds (sulphate of ammonia etc.) are rapidly oxidized to nitrate in the soil for use by plants. In very acid or poorly drained soils this oxidation does not occur: the ammonium accumulates, causing death of the plant roots and eventually of the whole plant. Legumes, which are plants of the pea and bean family, are able to convert nitrogen from the air into nitrate in the soil. Such plants are excellent for improving sandy soils, to which they are well adapted. Nitrogen may be applied to the soil as ammonium salts (sulphate of ammonia, nitram) or as nitrate of soda or nitrate of potash.

## Phosphorus

Phosphorus (as phosphate) is used to make sugars in the plant and to promote root growth. Phosphate, like nitrate, is not held on clay but it combines with calcium to form the very insoluble calcium phosphate. This is slowly made available to plants by the activity of soil micro-organisms, but in very alkaline (limy) soils the phosphate may not be made available in sufficient quantity even when present in very large amounts. Superphosphate of lime or triple superphosphate are the usual materials for supplementing phosphate in soil and the addition of organic matter will indirectly increase phosphate supply by stimulating micro-organism activity.

## Potassium

Potassium (potash) is also associated with the making of sugars and it particularly improves flowering, fruiting and sturdiness of plants. It is held on clay particles but is readily available to plant roots. Supplies may be supplemented by applying wood ash or sulphate of potash to the soil.

## Magnesium and iron

Magnesium and iron are both used in forming chlorophyll, the green substance which enables plants to make sugars. Like potassium they are metals and are held by clay particles for release to plant roots, but iron especially becomes unavailable in alkaline soils. Plants vary in their ability to take up iron, but susceptible plants become very pale or 'chlorotic' in limy soil. Iron can be added in a special, and expensive, organic form in such circumstances (see below, 'Coping with chalk soils'), but for normal purposes sulphate of iron and sulphate of magnesium (Epsom salts) can be applied to supplement these two minerals.

## Calcium

Calcium is required principally to stiffen cell-walls, the 'bones' of the plant. For this purpose it is only required in small quantities but calcium compounds have a more general role in modifying the acidity of the soil. The natural tendency of a soil is to become more acid as time passes. Calcium oxide (quicklime), calcium hydroxide (hydrated or slaked lime) and calcium carbonate (chalk or limestone) will neutralize the acidity.

Calcium also causes clay particles to stick together into larger crumbs, improving soil texture. When this improvement is required, but it is not desirable to make the soil more alkaline, the neutral mineral calcium sulphate (gypsum) can be used.

## SOIL TESTING

The pH of the soil can be measured quite easily using a soil-testing kit. More elaborate kits are also available for estimating the levels of major nutrients, providing useful information for the technically-minded gardener. Measurement of lesser nutrients, however, requires considerable practice to achieve reliable results. If micro-nutrient problems are suspected, a complete soil test at a professional laboratory is advisable. Such deficiencies are unlikely in Britain, however, unless the soil is either extremely acid, alkaline or deficient in organic matter, in which case treatment of the basic cause of the problem will result in a more lasting cure than will application of particular deficient nutrients.

## COPING WITH SANDY SOIL

The advantages of sandy soils have already been noted. Being very well drained they warm up early in the spring and can be cultivated easily at almost any time of year. They are therefore good for producing early crops. Sandy soils are almost always acid (except when they contain large amounts of crushed sea shells) and will support the many beautiful ericaceous plants (heathers, rhododendrons, etc.), as well as being suited to the making of fine lawns. Many attractive plants will grow well, but slowly, on sandy soils but, because they are dry and leached of nutrients, these soils are of little value for producing rapid, succulent growth such as is required for vegetables and annuals in general. Before these plants can be grown successfully, it is essential to improve the water-holding ability of the soil, to increase its nutrient content and, in the case of some vegetables, to overcome the acidity by heavy liming.

### Increasing water retention in sandy soil

Water holding can be increased by digging in clay when it is available: this practice of 'marling' was widely used in the eighteenth century to improve light farmland. It is usually more practical, however, to increase the supply of organic matter. Where supplies of manure are plentiful, dressings of 15–20kg/m$^2$ (30–40lbs/yd$^2$) would not be excessive for vegetable gardens. Garden compost is also invaluable, but where neither is available in quantity, straw, spent hops, shredded paper or sawdust may be composted with nitrochalk or with nitrate of soda or nitrate of potash and lime. 50–100kg (1–2cwt) of these materials per tonne of organic material will produce a rich manure-substitute for digging in. Many local authorities now produce composted green waste which is an excellent soil improver and often available at very low or no cost.

Mulches of compost 50–75mm (2–3in) deep between rows of vegetables and soft fruits will also conserve water and supply nutrients where they are most easily absorbed by the numerous surface-feeding roots. Such mulches should also smother weeds but if the composting has not been thorough the many weed seeds germinating in the mulch itself can be removed by hoeing or by spraying paraquat (see Chapter 3). Peat has been much used in the past as a soil improver but its use is now regarded as environmentally unsound.

Green manuring also improves the water-holding capacity of sandy soils. Quick-growing crops such as rape, mustard, rye grass and annual lupin are sown and, when well established or about to flower, a dug into the soil. It is even more beneficial, and the process is also easier if the top-growth is chopped roughly with a spade and dusted with lime (75–150g/m$^2$ or 2–4oz/yd$^2$) before digging. Annual lupin, clover and beans are especially valuable for the additional nitrogen which they supply to the soil.

### Timing of cultivation on sandy soil
All cultivations on sandy soil are best left until spring, allowing only sufficient time for firming and raking the soil before sowing and planting. This prevents nutrients being washed away by winter rains before they have served any useful purpose. During the growing season, too, quick-acting fertilizers are best applied in small, frequent doses to prevent waste.

### Irrigation of sandy soil
To make the greatest use of this carefully improved sandy soil it is well worth investing in irrigation equipment – trickle hose is more efficient in water use than overhead sprinklers – to

ensure continued growth of vegetables and fruit during the summer, remembering that permission from the Water Authority will be needed for this purpose. Permits can usually be obtained from the address to which water rates are sent. However, with the increase in water metering and the decrease of reliable water supplies when most needed in the garden, it also makes sense (economically and environmentally) to invest in waterbutts and other storage techniques.

This elaborate cultivation of sandy soil is only required where heavy yields of vegetables and fruit are sought. Ornamental plants, if wisely chosen, will grow slowly but surely without such care, although it is worth improving the soil to assist the establishment of new plants. Spring applications of general fertilizer in subsequent years will of course increase the rate of growth and hasten maturity but they are not necessary for the survival of plants.

## PLANTS FOR SANDY SOIL

There is no shortage of plants which will thrive on acid, sandy soils. Of the deciduous trees, oak, hawthorn, birch and chestnut immediately come to mind. These are represented not only by our native species, valuable though they may be, but also by numerous exotics, especially from North America. *Quercus coccinea* and *Q. rubra* (*borealis*), the scarlet and red oaks, are notable for autumn colour, as are the hawthorns from that same part of the world. *Crataegus crus-galli* and *C. phaenopyrum* are among the best hawthorns, the first brilliant but short-lived in autumn tints of orange and gold, the latter more richly purple-coloured and much longer-lasting in both leaf and fruit. Birches, too, offer autumn colour but are even more useful in winter for their beautiful trunks. Those of *Betula maximowicziana* are multi-coloured in cream, pink and white, *B. papyrifera* has one of the whitest barks, while our own

*B. pendula* in its various forms is also very beautiful. *Liquidambar styracifiua*, too, is renowned for autumn colour and although usually associated with moist sites (often gaining by reflection in lakes) it will grow on drier sites, colouring the more brilliantly on its starvation diet.

Another excellent tree for sandy soils is *Catalpa bignonioides*, the 'Indian bean' or 'Cigar tree'. On sand it grows relatively slowly and often assumes a picturesque outline. On richer soils, it grows very quickly and rather openly. It has no autumn colour, but its enormous pale green leaves and the fragrant white flowers produced in late summer more than compensate for this. The long 'beans' produced after the flowers, and which give the plant its common names, are not true beans of course – catalpa has no botanical affiliation with the *Leguminosae*, that great family which includes the beans and peas, as well as many plants of particular value on sandy soils.

The legumes as a family do well on sandy soils, being adapted to providing their own nitrogen supply to compensate for their impoverished situation. These remarks apply to legumes of all sizes: the tall *Robinia pseudoacacia*, *Gleditsia triacanthos* and *Sophora japonica*; the smaller laburnums, slender *Genista aetnensis* and silvery *Cytisus battandieri*; the ground-hugging *Genista hispanica* and *Cytisus* × *kewensis*. Tree lupins grow to a considerable age and stature on sand, while the somewhat tender *Coronilla glauca*, smothered in sweet-scented flowers for much of the winter, is more reliably hardy on dry, sandy soil than anywhere else.

Very free drainage also imparts hardiness to a wide range of other marginally hardy plants, whether grown for their silvery foliage (santolina, artemisia, cinerarea, centaurea), their flowers (ceanothus, cistus, salvia, phygelius) or both (romneya, perovskia, caryopteris, anthemis and *Convolvulus cneorum*).

It is not surprising that all the plants mentioned thus far, except some of the silver-leaved plants (which overcome the drought problem by reflecting much of the sunlight which would otherwise drain them of moisture), have thongy, unbranching roots which thrust deep into the soil to reach supplies of water. Because of this they do not transplant well and are best obtained as small, pot-grown specimens to enable them to establish with the minimum of root disturbance.

This is true, too, for many of the herbaceous plants which grow well on sand. Acanthus, limonium, crambe, echinops, eryngium, agapanthus and alstroemeria all transplant badly but, once established, will survive prolonged drought and contribute much to the garden in both leaf and flower.

Evergreens are not lacking either. Evergreen oak (*Quercus ilex*), holly, *Elaeagnus × ebbingei* and olearias of all shapes and sizes thrive on sand, while among the conifers cupressus, juniper and pine are equally tolerant. These three genera alone range from the darkest greens of *Cupressus sempervirens* or *Pinus nigra* to the blue and grey shimmer of *C. arizonica* or *P. wallichiana* (*griffithii*), from the majestic pines and tall feathery cypresses to low, ground-hugging junipers in various shades of green, gold, grey and glaucous blue. Like so many plants suited to sandy soils, the evergreens mentioned here (and the conifers in particular) resent disturbance and are best planted while small. This does not apply to the last major group of plants, the *Ericaceae*.

Ericaceous plants, most of which are evergreen, thrive on sand, it is true, but they usually inhabit wet or shaded habitats in which their fine superficial mass of fibrous roots will not suffer harm. In such situations, with acid soil conditions greatly reducing the breakdown of organic matter, a thick spongy blanket of peaty leafmould develops and in this the plants flourish. The family *Ericaceae* includes an enormous range of plants: the heaths (calluna, daboecia, erica) which require open situations away from the drip of trees, the trailing gaultheria and pernettya, which are equally at home in sun or shade, the more aristocratic kalmia, pieris and oxydendron, which in Britain are plants of thin woodland, and the great race of rhododendrons. This vast genus ranges from Himalayan mountainsides to sub-tropical jungles but, in general, the taller the species and the larger its leaf, the more easily it will be damaged by drying winds or direct sunlight. The rhododendrons are among the most beautiful plants for sandy soils but they must have an adequate supply of organic matter in – or on – the soil. A generous annual mulch of leaf-mould or other organic soil-improver is ideal.

## Fruit and vegetables on sandy soil

The most important points relating to the cultivation of fruits and vegetables on sand have already been made above – the main problems are that sandy soils are impoverished, excessively drained and acid.

Acidity is unimportant when growing flowers because many of the finest flowering plants actually benefit from or require acid soil, but fruits and vegetables are different. The brassicas, including cabbage, cauliflower, Brussels sprouts, radish, swede and other, less important, vegetables, are prone to club root, which is particularly serious on acid soil. Most tree fruits are also better on moderately alkaline soil. Raspberries are the exception among fruits in requiring acid soil and for the more adventurous gardener, blueberries grow on very acid soils, but both require adequate organic matter. Fortunately, excessive soil acidity is very easily overcome by adding lime.

If the problems of sandy soils are overcome by manuring, irrigation and liming, they have enormous advantages over other soil types for food production. They are easily worked at most times of the year and they warm up quickly in spring, so early crops can be produced. Historically, many of the most successful market gardens were deliberately sited on sandy soils for this reason.

Free drainage and light soil are especially useful for overwintering crops, such as broad beans, and for early sowing of peas, beans and other seeds, which would rot on heavier soils.

Marrows and tomatoes benefit from free drainage if water can be supplied, as do the deep-rooting onions and leeks, and maincrop roots, such as carrots and beet. Brassicas are less favoured, especially the Brussels sprout, which is traditionally a crop of heavy-clay loams, but if liming is attended to and nitrogen levels are topped up during the growing season, there is no reason why first-class crops of most brassicas should not be grown.

Fruit poses less of a problem. Strawberries and raspberries will grow well on acid soils and most bush fruits will tolerate mildly acid conditions. Tree fruits may lack vigour on sand. They should be grown on the more vigorous rootstocks and in bare ground rather than in grass – or at least with a wide 1–2m (3–6ft) diameter circle of bare ground around each tree to reduce the competition from grass. All nutrients are likely to be deficient, so the addition of a balanced fertilizer is important. Plums require more nitrogen than other fruits and this can be supplied by nitrochalk in spring. Plums, cherries and other stone fruits also require adequate supplies of calcium. A particular problem associated with fruit growing on sandy soils is phosphate deficiency. If this is rectified by using basic slag or superphosphate of lime, rather than the newer triple superphosphate, it will help to counter not only phosphate deficiency, but also calcium deficiency and the associated acidity.

Free drainage and early warming make sandy soils suitable for the less common fruits, such as peaches and figs. Peaches require heavy applications of lime, preferably the slow-acting crushed limestone, for success. Figs, although less vigorous and more fruitful on poor soil, will require a light application of potash each year and watering in dry summers for heavy cropping.

Pessimists may claim that all soils have some disadvantages for kitchen gardening and there is some truth in the accusation. But the disadvantages of sandy soils are more easily overcome than those of other soils to provide a growing medium suitable for adventurous gardening.

## COPING WITH CHALK SOIL

It seems paradoxical that chalk soils, thought by many people to be the worst possible soils for gardening, should have our richest variety of native flowering plants. The paradox is easily understood when one realizes that the richness of native species occurs in open areas of fine grass away from tall trees and away, even, from coarse, tussocky grasses. The lack of soil fertility allows many non-competitive plants to flourish. If fertility is increased, tall plants invade and the weaker species of wild flowers quickly fade away.

It was long thought that chalk soils were excessively dry. We now realize that chalk is a very efficient sponge, soaking up and holding large quantities of water but it is too hard a rock for roots to penetrate, so much of the water is unavailable for plants. The roots of beech, ash, viburnum, hazel and other woody plants, unable to penetrate the chalk, form a dense shallow mat, quickly exhausting the surface water supply and suppressing other plants.

### Increasing water availability in chalk soil

Breaking up the chalk by pick-axe, tractor-drawn subsoiling tines or explosives, depending on the scale of operations, and incorporating organic matter into the deeper layers allows roots to penetrate the chalk mass. A much larger volume of water in the chalk can therefore be exploited and plant growth is enormously improved. Because of the alkaline, well-drained nature of chalk, humus breaks down rapidly so additions of organic matter should be frequent and heavy.

Although the chalk itself holds water the light soil drains rapidly and, as chalk areas are in the dry south-east of the country, irrigation is of enormous benefit, especially in the vegetable garden. As in sandy areas, all methods of water conservation and storage will reap rich rewards.

## PLANTS FOR CHALK SOIL

The choice of ornamental plants is very wide and the main warning would be against growing those plants which are susceptible to chlorosis (paling of the leaves caused by excess lime). Most important of this group are the *Ericaceae* as a whole, although strangely the strawberry tree, *Arbutus unedo*, flourishes on chalk. The list of plants to avoid would also include most of the brooms and many plants grown for autumn colour: American oaks, amelanchier, liquidambar, Japanese maple, witch hazel and a few others though here the problem is more of drought than alkalinity. On deeper soils over chalk these plants will grow perfectly well.

There is no shortage of autumn colour on chalk, however. *Acer ginnala*, *A. griseum* and *A. cappadocicum* replace the more fastidious Japanese maple. *Acer ginnala* is the smallest of the trio. It is attractive in flower and when the young fruits assume a reddish tinge, as well as colouring brilliantly in autumn. On *A. griseum* the pink-tinted spring foliage is as delightful as its stronger autumn colour, while the peeling orange bark is attractive throughout the year. Norway maple, *A. platanoides*, also colours well but its dense, spreading canopy makes it less suitable for small gardens. The sumachs *Rhus typhina* and *R. glabra* are among the most brilliant of autumn foliage plants, whether one grows the species or the finer textured cut-leaved forms. The latter sucker less freely in the early years, an advantage in small gardens, and all are attractive in winter with their 'stag's horn' branch structure.

*Rosaceae* is a family with many genera which grow satisfactorily on chalk. Crab-apples, cherries, mountain ash and cotoneaster provide a wide range of plant forms from vigorous trees to low ground-covers, and their autumn colour of foliage or fruits is usually supplemented – or even surpassed – by their spring flowers. *Malus sargentii*, a low shrubby tree, and the taller *M. tschonoskii* are especially colourful in autumn foliage with 'Dartmouth Crab', 'Golden Hornet' and 'John Downie' for fruit. All are attractive in flower, but *M. coronaria* 'Charlottae' and *M. floribunda* excel where flower is of primary importance. Among the cherries *Prunus sargentii* has the most brilliant autumn colour, but it is not suitable for very shallow chalk soils. The great range of Japanese flowering cherries colour moderately well in the autumn while *P. subhirtella* 'Autumnalis' has autumn interest of a different kind. This graceful, small-leaved tree flowers unceasingly from November to April. The common mountain ash, *Sorbus aucuparia*, is more successful on acid soils than on chalk but *S. hupehensis* grows well on chalk. The small, glaucous leaves and white, long-lasting fruits of this species are especially effective against a dark background. Cotoneasters are excellent plants for chalk. Treelike cotoneasters, such as *Cotoneaster frigidus*, *C. salicifolius* or *C. × watereri*, large shrubs such as *C. conspicuus*, *C. franchetii* or *C. simonsii* and the ground-hugging *C. congestus*, *C. dammeri*, *C. prostratus* or trailing varieties of *C. salicifolius* offer a range of form and foliage texture equalled by few other plants. Most produce bright red fruits in great quantity, but *C.* 'Exburiensis' and a few others have yellow fruits, which are not only more conspicuous but also much more persistent.

Viburnums in general also grow well on chalk and perhaps the easiest way to advise on selection is to name the two species which are not very successful. The tall and large-leaved *V. rhytidophyllum* and magnificent, horizontally branched *V. plicatum* will grow on alkaline soils but die or look very distressed if grown in a dry situation. They are not worth growing on dry, chalky soils but *V. × rhytidophylloides* is a good substitute for the first named.

Among taller flowering trees, *Aesculus* (horse chestnut) in general, *Davidia involucrata*, *Paulownia tomentosa* and *Koelreuteria paniculata* are suitable. The last three not only survive on chalk but will usually produce their delightful flowers several years earlier on a spartan diet than on rich, well-watered soil. Lilacs, including the tree lilac *Syringa reticulata* (*amurensis japonica*), privets (which much-maligned genus includes the scented *Ligustrum quihoui* and glossy, evergreen, late-flowering *L. lucidum*) and *Cercis siliquastrum* extend the range from trees to large shrubs. Two other shrubs worthy of special mention are *Photinia serrulata* and *Kolkwitzia amabilis*. The former, an attractive, evergreen relative of the hawthorns, is most notable for its bright red young foliage. It will grow on chalk (though not on shallow chalk soils) to produce much the same effect that one associates with *Pieris formosa* on acid soils. *Kolkwitzia amabilis* not only grows on chalk but is only really worth growing on chalk. On rich soils it is an undistinguished, rather leggy shrub of no special merit. On chalk it is more compact and forms a large dome smothered for many weeks in early summer with pink, tubular flowers over pale green, soft, hairy foliage. In autumn the foliage turns crimson-red and again the colouring is most pronounced on chalk.

Many evergreen plants are well suited to chalk. Box and yew are native to the chalk downs. Cedar, evergreen oak (*Quercus ilex*) and the smaller *Phillyrea decora*, much loved in the last century, are excellent in large gardens. The scale-leaved conifers such as chamaecyparis, cupressus, juniper and thuja (as opposed to needle-leaved pines, spruces and firs) grow well on chalk whether as tall, columnar trees, hedges or low, weed-smothering shrubs. Photinia, privets, viburnums and cotoneasters mentioned already as flowering or fruiting shrubs, also include many evergreen species, while under 'cherry' one might include the Portugal laurel *Prunus lusitanica*, an excellent, dark, glossy green shrub which also flowers profusely. Bay (*Laurus nobilis*) is less hardy than the superficially similar laurel but will grow to make a very large tree on well-drained soil in the south of England. A great many other ever-'greens', such as rosemary, lavender, teucrium, santolina and other aromatic and grey-leaved plants, also flourish particularly well on well-drained alkaline soil.

Early bulbs (using the term 'bulb' in its widest sense) also benefit from free drainage and rapid warming of the soil on chalk. Winter aconite, *Anemone blanda*, crocus in general, *Iris reticulata*, *Narcissus juncifolius*, most tulips, hyacinths and scillas come into this category. Cultivated tulips and hyacinths do not produce such large flowers as on rich soils but they settle down to make long-lived clumps. Narcissus in general do well on chalk, except for a few, such as *N. cyclamineus*. Snowdrops survive but do not increase rapidly unless the soil is reasonably moist. Lilies are generally poor, except *Lilium martagon*, which tolerates chalk, and *L. candidum*, which flourishes. Two surprises are *Fritillaria meleagris* and *Leucojum aestivum*, both naturally plants of the waterside but which survive and increase gradually, even in dry shady places. Among the late bulbs which flower more freely after the summer drought they are likely to experience on chalk are *Nerine bowdenii*, *Sternbergia lutea*, *Zephyranthes rosea* and *Crinum × powellii*. *Schizostylis*, on the other hand, definitely requires a moist situation and is unsatisfactory on chalk unless a source of water is available.

Herbaceous plants in general will grow well on chalk although some (hosta, ligularia, many primulas, phlox, montbretia) will not survive unless the soil is moist, and many will not flourish unless the soil is of reasonable depth and fertility. For chalk soils dry enough and shallow enough to constitute a real problem, there is still a wide range of herbaceous plants from which to choose. With classics such as Graham Stuart Thomas's *Perennial Garden Plants* (Frances Lincoln, 2004) and Beth Chatto's *The Dry Garden* (Sagapress, 1998) there is little necessity to describe plants in detail here, but the following can be recommended for the most difficult situations: acanthus, alstroemeria, centaurea, *Cephalaria tatarica*, dianthus (pinks) of all kinds, *Dictamnus albus*, echinops, eryngium, *Filipendula hexapetala* (other filipendulas require very moist soils), gypsophila, *Iris unguicularis*, *I. pallida* and its forms, *Limonium latifolium, Nepeta × faassenii* (catmint), *Papaver orientalis, Pulsatilla vulgaris,* romneya, scabious, sedums of all kinds and verbascum.

In common with plants recommended for dry situations, many of these plants have deep, thongy roots and do not transplant well. Acanthus, alstroemeria, dictamnus, limonium and romneya are particularly difficult in this respect.

Also of great value on the driest, thinnest chalk soils are many low evergreens often treated as alpines. Arabis, aubrieta (including the neatly variegated forms of both), iberis, dianthus, helianthemums and perennial wallflowers (*Erysimum* 'Harpur Crewe', 'Moonlight', 'Bowles Mauve', etc.) will remain as compact, free-flowering and long-lived cushions on dry chalky soils whereas they outgrow their usefulness within two or three years on more fertile soils.

## Fruit and vegetables on chalk soil

In some respects chalk and sandy soils are similar. Both are poor and dry so measures such as spring cultivation, irrigation and frequent light application of nutrients recommended for sandy soils apply equally here.

There are important differences, however. Sandy soils are acid; chalk is very alkaline. Sandy soils are deep and easily worked whereas chalk soils are often shallow and overlie solid chalk.

Because they are alkaline, chalk soils do not usually require liming. Deep soils over chalk may become acid but such soils are not problems and so are outside the scope of the present paragraph. On very shallow soils small pieces of chalk can often be seen lying on the surface, or during cultivation, in which case lime is certainly not required. Such soils are likely to be deficient in phosphate, which becomes unavailable in alkaline conditions, so the use of triple superphosphate rather than the traditional (but also alkaline) basic slag or single superphosphate is advisable.

The shallow nature of chalk soils is a great disadvantage. Deep digging to break up the chalk and incorporation of organic matter in the lower layers without bringing the chalk to the surface is of enormous and long-lasting benefit. Even so, the lumpy consistency of chalk-strewn soil will discourage the growing of maincrop carrots and other root vegetables in favour of globe or stump-rooted varieties. Brassicas present no problem as long as top-dressings of nitrogen are given at intervals throughout the growing season to stimulate leaf growth. Leeks and onions also benefit from added nitrogen.

The majority of culinary herbs succeed admirably on chalk. Sage, thyme, hyssop, horehound, rosemary and many others make compact, long-lived bushes as a result of the dry conditions. Parsley and mint are the two main herbs which really do not grow well. Parsley is best grown in the vegetable garden where thorough soil improvement is routine while mint is better in its own carefully prepared and enriched bed – both for its own sake and to curb its wandering tendencies.

Chalk soils will grow most fruits satisfactorily if phosphate levels can be maintained. The one exception is raspberry which is much better on acid soil, but even this can be grown well if mulched generously and watered when the fruits are swelling.

Peaches and figs are particularly well suited to chalk soils.

## COPING WITH HEAVY CLAY SOIL

### Draining clay soil

Difficulties in coping with clay are exacerbated by the fact that, having been deposited by water, it usually occurs in flat, low-lying areas from which the removal of surplus water is difficult. Some form of drainage is almost essential, however, if the garden is to have a reasonable lawn and/or vegetable plot. The best form of drainage in the long term is to use tile drains in trenches back-filled with coarse gravel and leading to a deep soakaway or, ideally, to a ditch. Installation of a durable system of tile drains is a skilled and, without the right machinery, exceedingly arduous undertaking. On a large scale it is best left to an agricultural contractor. In small gardens the foundations of the house, terrace and paths, and the network of trenches made for sewers, electricity, water and other services will frequently serve to drain the garden. Paradoxically, draining a clay soil will increase the amount of water available to plants by stimulating deeper rooting into the soil.

## Improving the texture and structure of clay soil

All soil cultivations should be aimed at improving soil texture and structure. Incorporation of organic material, especially strawy stable manure, and green manuring with annual rye grass will improve soil structure. Sand does not improve the texture substantially unless incorporated in sufficient quantity to form a significant proportion of the soil – sufficient for each sand grain to be in contact with others, thus forming large spaces for water to drain through. Used in the necessary quantity, sand is expensive, but some small gardens have been improved in this way, working a 50mm (2in) layer of sand and a 50mm (2in) layer of compost into the soil with a rotary cultivator to produce a soil of John Innes potting compost consistency. Bonfire ashes, weathered coal ash, burned clay (produced by heaping lumps of clay around the hot ash of a bonfire), fine brick rubble and other coarse materials will also gradually improve the clay.

## Raising the level of clay soil

These materials also serve to raise the level of the soil above its surroundings, which also improves drainage. The raising can be exaggerated in the vegetable garden by sinking the paths to act, in winter, as open drainage channels leading to a soakaway. Near the house, where walls and steps are appropriate, the change in level may be enhanced still further to create raised beds. Most bulbs and alpines flourish in a

150–300mm (6–12in) layer of very well-drained soil over heavy clay as they have access to adequate water supplies without risk of rotting. At a greater distance from the house, drainage may be improved locally by digging a pond to create a really wet area (which will need to be lined or puddled if it is to retain water in summer) and throwing up the soil thus produced to make a well-drained mound.

**Cultivation of clay soil**
Timing of cultivation is very important. Digging when the soil is dry is nearly impossible. When the clay is wet, treading or cultivation will quickly ruin its structure. Ideally digging should be done in autumn when the soil is just moist, leaving the soil in large lumps for frost to work on over winter. When digging, one should avoid taking too big a spadeful of soil; it is unnecessarily hard work. A strong stainless steel spade is a good investment and the spade should be cleaned frequently during use. In the spring the soil should break down easily into a good tilth and one should be careful to work only in dry weather, or preferably from the path or a scaffold plank, to avoid damaging the soil structure developed by winter freezing.

Stainless steel spade and just-moist soil or not, the digging of clay soil is very hard work and should be avoided where possible by using permanent ground-covering plants, of which a great many are available. An adequate system of paths and paving around the house, vegetable garden and other frequently travelled routes will save both soil structure and footwear in wet weather and if the path system allows bicycles, tricycles, roller skates, etc., to be used, banishing children from the lawn during the wettest periods of the year is less punitive.

Two other miscellaneous but important points must be mentioned before dealing with specific plants: slugs and planting – especially where not to plant.

## Slugs

Slugs are a particular problem on wet, clay soils not only because of their numbers but because the many splendid foliage plants which grow so well on clay are the first to be attacked – and ruined – by slug activity. It is possible to trap slugs under slates or orange peel, etc., to deter them with rings of sand or sharp ashes around susceptible plants or to supress them with meta-bran preparations. Since the recent introduction of methiocarb, however, the use of this material (obtained commercially as 'Draza') to kill slugs has largely superseded older remedies.

## Planting on clay soil

Planting assumes special significance on clay because the soil is usually hard or sticky and lumpy. It is therefore difficult to work the soil at all effectively among the roots of new plants. To overcome this problem it is advisable to have a reliable source of prepared soil on hand especially for this purpose but a source which is not too different from the native soil. The vegetable garden is one obvious source. If soil is raked off rather than dug out it will be perfect for planting. Molehills are a second source for small quantities of soil, but not a source to be encouraged or relied upon. When extensive planting is anticipated it is advisable to cover a patch of bare soil with a 50mm (2in) mulch of compost and to cover this with polythene sheeting to keep out rain. Protected in this way from freezing or waterlogging, the soil will remain in excellent condition for mixing with its mulch and using in planting holes. Whichever of these methods is used, the planting soil is largely of garden origin. This overcomes problems which plants have in extending their roots from peat or other quite foreign material into the solid clay.

Where not to plant is a very controversial subject. The dry summers of 1975 and 1976 first drew widespread attention to the potential problem of extensive shrinkage of clay and damage to buildings on clay soil. Tree roots were held to blame, unfairly in many instances, for the damage thus caused. Because of its chemical and physical properties described earlier in this chapter, clay tends to swell when wetted and to shrink when dried. Studies of very heavy clays have shown that whole fields will rise a centimetre when a centimetre of rain falls, then sink a centimetre as the water evaporates again. Such soils are obviously unsuitable for building purposes and damage can be expected in very wet or very dry weather regardless of whether the vegetation evaporating the water is grass, cabbages or trees. It must also be remembered that removal of long-established trees on shrinkable clay soils can also cause soil levels to rise and this can result in more structural damage than clay shrinkage. In new construction the problem is now recognized and avoided by deeper foundations or raft construction. In older properties on clay soils particularly, it is obviously advisable to avoid having willows, poplars, ash or other large trees with extensive root systems near the house. There is also much to be said for a wide terrace sloping away from the house to reduce soil movement beneath the foundations, but to banish small laburnums and mountain ash to the farthest corners of the garden or to surround the house in a great sea of concrete is as foolish as it is futile. It would be better by far to leave the clay lands to Brussels sprouts and oak forest and to build on more stable soils, but this advice is within the realms of politics, not gardening, and will certainly go unheeded.

## PLANTS FOR CLAY SOIL

The main recommendation in selecting plants for clay soils would be to avoid the plants most strongly recommended for sand or chalk! This still leaves an enormous range to choose from.

Assuming that the clay is reasonably well drained, all the tree-sized maples, the horse chestnuts (shrubby and tall), birches, ash, larch, oaks and limes will flourish. In lower, wetter positions this list must be reduced, but red maple (*Acer rubrum*), river birch (*Betula nigra*) and pin oak (*Quercus palustris*), among the most beautiful of their respective genera, are obvious candidates for such situations. *Liquidambar styraciflua* may be added and *Nyssa sylvatica* must be added. Although all these trees have good autumn colour, the brilliant red of the slender, slow growing nyssa is unbeatable. Alders and hazels, including the handsome *Corylus colurna*, are fast-growing, often picturesque trees for waterside planting, while the two deciduous conifers *Metasequoia glyptostroboides* and *Taxodium distichum* add vertical accents and paler, more feathery foliage. One of the fastest-growing trees for wet positions is *Pterocarya fraxinifolia*, with bold, ash-like leaves and a suckering habit which can be controlled or exploited as required. Faster still, of course, are poplars and willows.

In planting trees of any kind on heavy clay soil care must be taken not to create a sump for water in the planting hole, and use of organic soil improvers which might damage roots by fermentation in waterlogged conditions should be avoided. The nineteenth-century practice of planting trees on a mound, rather than in a pit, has much to commend it.

Dire warnings have already been given about their possible effects on buildings, but this need not prevent such delightful species as *Salix alba* 'Chermesina', *S. daphnoides*, *S. elaeagnos* and *S. purpurea* being grown for their decorative winter stems. Regular stooling of the plants will control root extension as well as providing the brightest stem colours. *S. matsudana* 'Tortuosa' has winter interest of a different kind: its slender spiralling twigs. These erupt in spring into a froth of narrow, pale green leaves, also contorted. This is one of the larger willows, but it can be stooled to keep it small. Indeed it is so easily replaced by rooting hardwood cuttings that it can be highly recommended for temporary occupation of even the smallest garden. Similar comments on the stooling of potentially large trees apply to *Populus* × *candicans* 'Aurora' and *P.* 'Serotina Aurea', except that here large leaves rather than bright stems are the objective in stooling.

Thus used, the willows and poplars associate well with lower shrubs. *Cornus alba* and *C. stolonifera* have a variety of forms with red or olive green stems, white or yellow variegation and, in all cases, superb autumn and winter colour from leaves and stems. *Ilex verticillata*, a rarely seen but easily grown deciduous holly, has almost black stems to highlight the colours of cornus, and its own brilliant scarlet berries on leafless winter stems. The holly is dioecious, so at least one male plant should be included in any group of female plants. *Clethra alnifolia* is grown for its sweetly scented flowers produced in late summer and, like the holly and cornus, will grow even in soil which is occasionally inundated. *Aronia arbutifolia* and *A. melanocarpa* provide flowers, fruit and autumn colour in generous measure, as do the larger but slower-growing hawthorns *Crataegus crusgalli*, *C.* × *lavallei* and *C. prunifolia*. Of shrubs grown primarily for their flowers, one might single out *Rubus* 'Tridel', *Viburnum opulus*, *V.* × *bodnantense* (which flowers in winter) and the weigelas as flourishing especially well in very moist, but not inundated, soils.

For evergreen interest, hollies of all kinds and the distinctive umbrella pine, *Sciadopitys verticillata*, are especially good but many of the firs (*Abies concolor*, *A. grandis*, etc.), Lawson's cypress, cotoneaster, and pines will grow in clay if waterlogging is not a serious problem.

If autumn and winter interest have been emphasized in the selection of shrubs it is because of the spectacular array of spring and summer effects which can be obtained using herbaceous plants on clay soils. There is a bonus here in that, perhaps because of the abundant water supply, even those plants grown primarily for their flowers often have excellent, decorative foliage. Likewise most foliage plants have the added interest of flowers.

*Lysichitum americanum* and *L. camtschatcense* are good examples to start the year. Yellow and white spathes respectively give way to large, mottled green leaves in the summer. *Caltha palustris* (marsh marigold) and closely related trollius are also early and bright with finer-textured but still attractive foliage. As spring advances so do primulas, *Primula rosea* and *P. denti-culata* first, then armies of candelabra primulas (*P. beesiana*, *P. bulleyana*, *P. chungensis*, *P. japonica*, *P. pulveru-lenta*, etc.) with the yellow *P. florindae*, beautifully scented, taking the genus into high summer. *Ajuga reptans*, grown for its purple or variegated leaves as much as for its flowers, has spikes of blue above its ground-hugging foliage in spring. Irises, such as *I. kaempferi*, *I. laevigata*, *I. sibirica* and our native *I. pseudacorus* come later with strong, sword-like foliage. The blue meconopsis help to cool the bright colours of primulas but are more difficult than most other plants listed here. They require a moist, peaty soil over the clay and will usually rot if planted straight into heavy soil. *Ligularia clivorum* and the unpronounceable *L. przewalskii* both have purple-tinged foliage and yellow-orange flowers, but the former is as robust as the latter is stately. These ligularias need a sheltered or partially shaded position as they will otherwise wilt in a very dejected manner on hot days even if freely supplied with water at the roots.

*Lythrum salicaria* takes the flower season into late summer, which is just as well: the brilliant pink of 'Robert', 'Firecandle' and other modern cultivars would probably explode on contact with the yellows and oranges mentioned above. A great advantage of heavy, wet, soil is that it permits the display of flowers to continue unabated through high summer into autumn. Hemerocallis have a long season if chosen carefully. The paler and later ones such as 'North Star' associate well with *Campanula lactiflora* and border phlox, both of which flower most satisfactorily and over the greater part of late summer in moist soils. *Lobelia cardinalis*, *Cimicifuga racemosa*, *C. ramosa* and *Gentiana asclepiadea*, a patriotic association of red, white and blue, take the flowering season well on into autumn.

Almost all of these plants have foliage interest as well as flowers, but other plants are grown specifically for their foliage. Stripy *Acorus calamus*, brilliant yellow *Filipendula ulmaria* 'Aurea', huge *Gunnera manicata*, hosts of hosta, darmera (pelti-phyllum), podophyllum, rheum, rodgersia and tellima are among the more important plants: 'spectacular' is not an over-statement in the case of gunnera or rheum, expecially when the latter produces its tall creamy inflorescences. Ferns and water associate naturally and one can recommend ferns in general for wet clay soils without elaborating further on the range of heights and textures which this one small word encompasses.

Bulbs in general are not amenable to cultivation in wet situations but snowdrops and many narcissi, especially *N. cyclamineus*, grow and increase more readily in moist than in dry soils. Snake's head fritillary, *Fritillaria meleagris*, Loddon lily, *Leucojum aestivum*, and the earlier-flowering snowflake, *L. vernum*, will grow almost in water, as will the tall blue camas-sias. If the wet clay is overlain with a layer of leafy or peaty soil, then a wide range of lilies can be added to the list, notably *Lilium canadense*, *L. pardalinum* and *Cardiocrinum giganteum*.

## Fruit and vegetables on clay soil

If attention is paid to improving drainage, texture and struc-ture, clay soils are retentive and fertile, eminently suitable for the majority of vegetables and fruits. Liming, as required by brassicas (cabbages, Brussels sprouts, cauliflower, etc.) assists in improving the soil structure and the annual preparation of manure-filled trenches or ridges for runner-beans, tomatoes, marrows, celery, etc., will gradually improve the whole plot, allowing the cultivation of peas, onions and other vegetables liable to rot on heavy soil. Clay warms up only slowly in the spring so early crops are not possible without the aid of cloches and autumn sowing of broad beans etc is inadvisable. Heavy soil and high slug populations can also reduce the success of long-rooted and late-maturing carrots, parsnips, maincrop potatoes, etc., so stump-rooted and mid-season varieties should be grown at least until regular cultivation has eliminated these problems. Tree fruits tend to excessive vigour on fertile clay and should be grown in grass to ensure reliable cropping of high-quality fruit. Planting on a slight mound to prevent waterlogging of the crown in winter is advisable. Apart from these minor problems there should be little difficulty in growing good crops of vegetables and fruit on clay.

# 3. Garden Dereliction

When starting on a garden there is frequently an inheritance of rubbish to be dealt with. In new gardens this will consist of builders' rubbish: bricks, half-used cement bags, wire, wood and similar debris. In older gardens household rubbish – old prams, bottles, mattresses etc. – add to the air of dereliction created by cracked, uneven paths, overgrown rockeries, leaking or stagnant ponds and unsightly improvised sheds.

Weeds and overgrown shrubs create further problems, sometimes reducing a garden to impenetrable jungle. The treatment of overgrown shrubs and borders requires careful consideration and, since such problems arise in well-maintained as well as in derelict gardens, that consideration is given separately in Chapter 4. Weed control is dealt with in this chapter, however, and it will be useful as a preliminary to introduce a range of herbicides.

## HERBICIDES

Herbicides are 'plant killers', not merely 'weedkillers', so an understanding of their uses and limitations is essential before they can be safely employed in the garden. Given that understanding they can be of enormous benefit in garden reclamation.

### Sodium chlorate
Sodium chlorate sterilizes the soil and will kill any plants growing in the treated area. It is a cheap and very effective herbicide for drives and terraces. Unfortunately it will wash off paving and through soil, remaining effective for a year or more, so it must not be used anywhere near desirable plants. Clothing wetted with sodium chlorate spray is rendered highly inflammable, so great care is needed in application.

## Paraquat/Diquat

Paraquat and Diquat are made completely inactive on contact with soil, so they have no persistent effect. Their action is to desiccate any tissue with which they come into contact, so a drench of paraquat or diquat will kill annual weeds and scorch the tops of perennial weeds. Woody plants are protected by their bark but care is still required when spraying around thin-barked trees such as young birch and cherry, especially in spring. Minor drifting of spray will mark plants but not damage them severely. They are so ephemeral in effect that ground cleared of annual weeds can be safely planted or sown within 24 hours. However, these chemicals will desiccate *any living tissue*, including lung's, digestive systems and kidneys. There is no antidote so they must be used with the greatest possible caution and kept out of reach of children. Formulations for amateur use are safer than those used by professional growers but, as with all chemicals, they must still be used with caution and according to manufacturer's instructions. Once sprayed on leaves or ground they are safe, and rain, even within an hour or so of spraying, will not seriously reduce their efficiency.

## 2-4D and 2-4-5T

2-4D (used in many lawn weedkillers) and 2-4-5T (brush-wood killer) are translocated herbicides; that is, they can be sprayed on the leaves of a plant and will move through the plant to growing points and roots, causing the whole plant to twist, wither and eventually die. 2-4D is the weaker chemical. Used at the correct rate it is an important lawn weedkiller, causing broad-leaved weeds to die, while leaving grasses unharmed. At two or three times this rate it can be used as a total herbicide, killing most annual and perennial weeds. 2-4-5T is stronger and is used to kill brambles, seedling trees and other woody growth. Both these herbicides are persistent, so several months must elapse before treated ground can be replanted. Great care must be taken to use a coarse spray on an absolutely calm day. Fine droplets will drift considerable distances in a slight breeze and can seriously damage crops, especially tomatoes, cucumbers and marrows. Mowings from treated lawns can be composted, but they should not be used fresh as a mulch.

## Aminotriazole

Aminotriazole (Amitrole) is also translocated but is especially active against grasses. It can be used to kill unwanted herbaceous vegetation among woody plants with a considerable margin of safety or, at higher doses, to eradicate herbaceous and woody plants together. Like 2-4D it is persistent and slow-acting. Several months must elapse before replanting can safely proceed.

A proprietary mixture of amitrole, 2-4D and diuron is sold for use on paths and drives. It will keep hard surfaces free of weeds for up to a year.

## Glyphosate

Glyphosate (Roundup) is a very useful herbicide for clearing vegetation. Sprayed on leafy growth, it is translocated throughout the sprayed plants and will kill them in three to six weeks. Like paraquat, however, it is inactivated on contact with soil. Sowing or planting can therefore occur within 24 hours of spraying. Glyphosate can be very effective in the control of couch-grass, creeping thistle and other pernicious weeds if used correctly. It is important that the chemical penetrates plant tissues so spraying should take place early in the morning or, ideally, on a calm, humid evening. Spraying in hot, drying conditions greatly reduces its effectiveness. Control of weeds with waxy surfaces (especially ground elder) is improved by physically damaging the leaves, with a rake or by trampling, or by covering the infested area with polythene sheet for a few days to force soft growth, before spraying. As a directed spray it can be used to kill these perennial weeds among desirable plants with a high degree of safety. It is one of the safest herbicides to handle although, like all garden chemicals, it should be treated with respectful caution.

## Casoron

Used as directed by the manufacturer on clean ground, Casoron will prevent germination of weed seedlings among shrubs. It has limited use in reclaiming a derelict garden but can be very useful in keeping shrub borders free of weeds after reclamation, allowing efforts to be directed elsewhere in the restoration programme.

## Alternatives to chemical herbicides

This diverse range of chemicals can greatly accelerate the bringing back to order of a neglected garden and can greatly reduce the physical effort required. However, many people will have qualms about the possible environmental damage caused by the use of herbicides. Where there is a philosophical objection to their use, a flame gun or hoe may be used to destroy annual weeds and mulches will do much to prevent their re-appearance. A flame gun or a strimmer will remove the tops of perennial weeds and regular pulling or digging out will eventually achieve a weed-free garden, but at higher cost in physical effort and in financial terms if mulches are used. Covering areas of weed infestation with black polythene for a season will eradicate all but the most persistent weeds by excluding light and raising the temperature, but the short-term visual impact will not be very pleasing.

## COPING WITH A NEGLECTED GARDEN

There are two basic approaches to coping with a neglected garden. The first is the evolutionary approach, where the existing garden is generally satisfactory in its content but has been poorly maintained for a period of months or years.

Allowing the garden to develop, capitalizing on its assets and tackling the backlog of maintenance will produce a satisfying and mature garden in a short time. The second is the revolutionary approach where the existing garden has little to offer and/or its owners are impatient to see a transformation. In this case the garden may be obliterated and, perhaps with the assistance of a professional garden designer and/or landscape contractors, a new garden installed.

Of course the two approaches are extremes on a continuum. In a mature and generally satisfactory garden there will be some scope and need to modify the garden perhaps removing unwanted, labour-intensive features and simplifying an over-complicated layout. In a fresh-start garden it would be folly to eliminate the existing garden in its entirely without first seriously considering whether any of its contents might not contribute to the new design. In particular it is important to avoid a superficial and cosmetic fresh start. Rotavating a ground-elder, couch and bindweed infested garden and popping a few fashionable grasses into a smart new gravel mulch may transform the garden for a few weeks or months but it will then rapidly degenerate into a post-revolutionary problem garden.

Irrespective of its position in the evolutionary/revolutionary spectrum, therefore, the preliminary treatment of a neglected garden involves a combination of rubbish clearance and weed control. The particular methods used will depend on the size of the garden, its age and degree of neglect, on plans for its development and on the inclinations of its owners, particularly in respect of their willingness to use chemical and mechanical aids.

## The new garden

In an entirely new garden surface debris will be the main problem around the house, perhaps with rank vegetation elsewhere, particularly if the house was built on farmland neglected for some years before building began.

## Rubbish clearance

Unused cement, bitumen and other substances toxic to plants should be removed as promptly as possible. The soil beneath split cement bags is best consigned to an area designated for paths or other paved areas where it will cause less damage than on an intended lawn or flower bed. Sand and shingle may be spread over the soil, unless they are clean enough to be stockpiled for subsequent use. Bricks, wood, wire and other debris can be picked off the surface, then it is advisable to ask a contractor to cultivate the area around the house with a heavy duty rotary cultivator. This will bring more debris to the surface and even out ruts and humps caused by the builders. If terraces, paths, drive and other hard surfaces can be planned before this cultivation, the topsoil should be removed from these areas, leaving depressions into which bricks and other suitable material can go to provide hardcore and providing a supply of precious topsoil where most needed.

## Weed control

Even before rubbish is cleared it is worth spraying weedy areas with paraquat or diquat. Any perennial weeds which regrow can then be treated with 2-4D or glyphosate and, if moving-in operations mean a delay in developing the garden, as is often the case, an occasional spray of paraquat or diquat as crops of young weeds emerge will keep the ground free of weeds, an inestimable advantage when starting a garden. Alternatively the ground can be covered with a weed-suppressing geotextile mat, concealed beneath a layer of gravel or bulk mulch if appearance is important.

If perennial weeds are a serious problem, as is often the case where new houses have been built in an old garden or on farmland, it is worth spending a whole year eliminating problem weeds. The time thus spent will pay enormous dividends thereafter. When the ground has been cleared, cleaned and cultivated, grass can be established by seed or turf leaving borders and the kitchen garden to be more deeply dug and enriched before planting. This assumes that planting is to proceed gradually. If the whole garden is planned and planted in a single operation it is better to attend to borders first and then to establish the lawn, avoiding too much walking or wheelbarrowing across the young grass.

## The overgrown garden

For established gardens which have become mildly overgrown, perhaps as a result of neglect for the year or so during which the house was changing hands, undergoing alterations, etc., the first thought in restoration should be for the lawn.

The important points in reclaiming neglected lawns are that the height of the grass should be reduced gradually to avoid killing it completely and that, once it is established at its final height, it should be cut as often as possible – certainly once a week – to supress coarse grasses and encourage finer-leaved grasses. Initially the grass should be cleared of surface debris and cut with a heavy-duty rotary mower, (probably hired for the occasion, as a mower producing a better finish will be required for permanent use). The mower should be set as high as the blades will go, and mowings should be collected and burned (where permissible) or disposed of as green waste, rather than composted, as they are likely to be full of grass and weed seeds. Once cut, the lawn can be edged and the adjacent strip of border cleaned to prevent further invasion of grass and creeping lawn weeds into borders. At each subsequent cut of the lawn the mowing height can be reduced by one notch until after the third or fourth cut the lawn should be quite low and even, although perhaps not as thick and weed-free as one would desire. Regular maintenance can then proceed as outlined in the chapter on lawns.

*Weed control*

While the lawn is being brought back into good condition, the drive, paths and any other unplanted areas can be cleared of rubbish and sprayed, as necessary, with paraquat if annual weeds are the main problem or 2-4D, glyphosate or a proprietary mixture if perennial weeds have become established.

With the lawn and paths in good condition the garden will quickly assume a cared-for appearance and attention can be turned to cultivating beds and borders, using a combination of hand-weeding, herbicide spraying and replanting. The procedure is the same as for severely neglected gardens and is described below.

## The long-neglected garden

In long-neglected gardens, there may be an impenetrable mass of nettles, docks, thistles, brambles, tree suckers or seedlings and overgrown shrubs with little evidence of lawn, paths or other garden features. The main problem in such gardens is to bring some semblance of order without destroying the existing sense of maturity.

The easiest approach, of course, is to bring in heavy machinery, push all the vegetation and rubbish into heaps and burn it, leaving a bare expanse on which a new garden has to be created. It is less expensive, and in many ways more satisfactory, to proceed more slowly with the clearance and to retain the better and well-established plants to contribute to the final scene. Preservation can be overdone, of course. In a few cases the garden may be of sufficient historical interest to merit accurate reconstruction, but it is usually a matter of adapting an old and complicated layout to more modern and more easily maintained lines. Any plants which interfere with the new plan should be removed or perhaps moved to a new situation. Herbaceous borders may have a few treasures of old varieties but more often they will be full of thickets of golden rod or weedy Michaelmas daisies which are best consigned to the bonfire or green-waste bin to make way for more useful and more manageable plants.

*Cleaning top-growth*
The first stage in developing a severely neglected garden is to cut down all unwanted top-growth. In a small garden this may be done with a sharp bill-hook, secateurs and shears. Remember, though, that it is much easier to pull up unwanted tree seedlings (with assistance from a pick-axe if necessary) than it is to cut down the seedlings and be faced with the problem of removing them by pulling or spraying later on. In large gardens manual cutting may be supplemented by mechanical flails, chain saw, heavy rotary mower or other equipment but the use of such equipment should be preceded by preliminary exploration and conspicuous marking of the plants which are to be retained. The piles of debris resulting from this clearance should be collected and burned or removed from the site as work progresses.

*Weed control*
Vigorous new growth stimulated by this cutting back should be sprayed during calm, warm, humid weather with 2-4D, glyphosate or, if there is much woody growth, with 2-4-5T, taking great care that none of these materials drifts on to desirable plants. Two or three sprays over a year or more may be required to effect a complete kill but the first spray will drastically check the growth of unwanted plants and allow other garden work to proceed.

**Removing tree-stumps**
In most gardens the problem of tree-stump removal will occur to a greater or lesser extent. Stumps of saplings are easily removed by excavating a little soil and severing the roots with a mattock or parrotbills (long-handled pruners) until the stump can be pulled out. Stumps of 50–150mm (2–6in) trunk dia-

meter are more difficult but are best dealt with in the same way, taking care to throw excavated soil well clear of the stump so that it does not fall back in as the hole deepens. Stumps with trunk diameters greater than about 150mm (6in) pose real problems. They may be excavated by hand or severed with an axe and hoisted out by winch, but a week of arduous toil may be required to remove even a moderately sized stump.

Where space permits, mechanical means may be used to remove the stumps. A mechanical shovel or JCB will dig out small stumps in one movement. Stump-chippers will tear away at very large stumps, reducing them to a pile of chips in less than an hour. There is now a wide range of compact and folding machinery so access to even quite difficult sites is increasingly possible. The cost of hiring machinery may seem high, especially for small tasks where the expense of transporting men and machines to the site far outweighs the cost of the actual work, but when several stumps have to be dealt with, £100 spent on a few hours of contractors' time might well save months of backbreaking part-time effort.

Another possibility, of course, is to leave the stumps to rot away. If they can be lacerated with an axe and sprinkled thickly with ammonium sulphamate, the rotting will be hastened. Ivies or other trailing plants may be used to cover the stumps, tall plants to conceal them or rough grass and bulbs to disguise them, but in all cases the overall appearance of the garden must be borne in mind. A hummock of rockery or inappropriate blob of nasturtiums in the middle of a lawn will merely draw attention to the stump instead of concealing it.

Whichever method of stump removal is used some large roots and stump fragments will remain, giving rise to an annual crop of toadstools every autumn until the wood has entirely rotted away. Sweeping off and fragmenting the toadstools will remove the visual symptoms of decay but only patience will eradicate the cause.

## PLANNING THE GARDEN

During and after preliminary clearance the main lines of the garden will become apparent and garden planning can begin. Garden design is outside the scope of this book except to mention that a garden of simple outlines with a clear contrast of open lawns and densely planted borders will be most effective as well as easiest to maintain. Convulsively curved borders surrounding lawns peppered with trees, flower beds, urns, rockeries and scattered shrubs are irritating to the eye as well as bothersome to the edging shears. Obviously, if the plan drawn up for the garden exploits patterns of planting, open space and paths which already exist, the effort involved in making the garden will be reduced. If the existing pattern is the remains of a complicated garden layout, however, some alteration and streamlining will be inevitable, but the effort spent on grubbing up redundant shrubs and digging out paths will be well rewarded in subsequent ease of maintenance and in the improved appearance of the garden.

### Preserving plants

*The nursery bed*
All unwanted top-growth having been cleared, the next stage in many gardens is to prepare a nursery bed. This will be used as a temporary repository for plants moved from elsewhere in the garden and as a reception area for newly acquired plants, whether gifts or purchases. Excellent value although hardy plants undoubtedly are, the cost of completely restocking a garden becomes more formidable each year. Buying plants well in advance means not only that they are bought at this year's prices rather than next, but also, by the time their permanent situation is ready they may have multiplied tenfold or more. The size of the nursery bed will depend entirely on the intentions of the gardener, but it should be situated in an open posi-

tion which has been cleared of perennial weeds and should be of a size which can be maintained impeccably. A weedy nursery is only going to perpetuate garden problems.

The need for a clean site may pose difficulties but paradoxically a bed of nettles often provides a very suitable area. Nettles form a very thick root system and very dense top growth which crowd out most other weeds. They are so shallowly rooted, however, that a fork thrust nearly horizontally into the root mass and levered up will get rid of most of the colony, remnants being removed by subsequent forking. A month of fallow will allow residual weeds to show themselves and be dealt with, then the ground can be used as a nursery, secure in the knowledge that as nettles only flourish in loose, fertile soil, the best position has been chosen for new plants!

*Cleaning borders*
Once the nursery bed is ready, work can begin on clearing herbaceous borders or colonies of herbaceous plants in mixed borders. The task of clearing weeds from established herbaceous borders is nearly impossible, so it is better to make a fresh start. Emptying a border can be done at any time. Indeed, unless one is familiar with all the plants, there is much to be said for emptying it gradually over a whole season, digging up the plants as they finish flowering, throwing away those which are not wanted and planting small pieces of more desirable plants in the nursery. In this way one is assured of discovering all the plants in the border and if planting in the nursery is done systematically a calendar of flowering times is automatically recorded.

There is a temptation simply to keep a proportion of all the plants lifted, but this is not advisable. Large masses of a plant indicate that it spreads freely, so it is only necessary to keep a few small pieces for subsequent re-establishment whereas a single small clump of a particular plant in an old border indicates that the plant is long-lived but slow to increase – desirable attributes for low-maintenance gardens, so every scrap of the plant should be salvaged and used.

It is also necessary to keep a sense of proportion in deciding how many plants to save. The simple operation of lifting a few clumps of amenable perennials and producing from them several dozen healthy divisions makes good sense. The painstaking excavation and replanting of a deep-rooting and probably moribund rose bush when a vigorous new plant could be obtained for £5–£10 is questionable, but the balance between re-cycling and buying-in will depend on the sense of values of the individual garden owner.

## Plant division

Herbaceous plants vary enormously in habit but a great many of them have shoots clustered more or less tightly around an older core. If each flowered stem is carefully teased out it will be seen to have one or more new shoots at the base, complete with new root systems. Such plants are easily divided and a dozen or more small divisions occupy little space in the

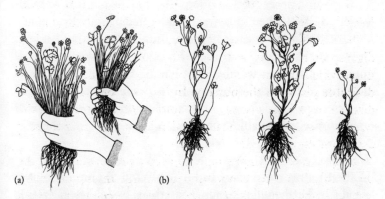

(a)                              (b)

Large clumps of herbaceous plants in an overgrown border will often harbour perennial weeds. Such clumps should be divided as in (a). Division into very small pieces – individual crowns where possible (b) – will then ensure that these weeds are not introduced into the nursery bed and will also rejuvenate old plants.

nursery. Other plants, such as hellebores, paeonies and heme-rocallis have a tougher root-stock and require a strong, sharp knife to divide them, although with patience these, too, may be separated into individual shoots for planting. Delphinium, lupin, gypsophila have numerous fleshy shoots attached to a single strong tap root. These plants are very difficult to divide and are best propagated by the rooting of cuttings obtained by snapping off the young shoots in spring. Plants vary in the ease with which they may be divided and a few may be lost through failure to recognize particular growth habits and requirements, but the losses are minute compared to the gain derived from a well-stocked nursery bed.

Lifting plants during or immediately after flowering and pulling them into small pieces is not the way to deal with herbaceous borders normally, but for renovating a garden it is a very satisfactory procedure. The small soil-less divisions are unlikely to carry any perennial weeds with them, and if the occasional fragment of bindweed does appear in the nursery it is easily dealt with by digging deeply to extricate the newly introduced pest.

The same procedure, incidentally, may be applied to bulbs which, if lifted when in flower, shaken free of soil, divided and replanted at once in their new situation, will re-establish with only a slight check, even though they may appear to die off more rapidly than usual after their move. Moving bulbs in flower is particularly useful when it is necessary to sort out old clumps of mixed daffodils, for example, into planned groups or to eliminate undesirable types.

### Hardwood cuttings
In the autumn, the nursery bed may be used to propagate many shrubs by hardwood cuttings. Forsythias, buddleias, flowering currants, deutzias, weigelas, potentillas, cornus, philadelphus – indeed most of the commoner garden shrubs – root readily if well-ripened shoots are inserted with about two-thirds of their

length below soil level soon after leaf-fall. Shoots of 200–300mm (8–12in) inserted 150–200mm (6–8in) deep are ideal. Careful lifting in late winter will reveal a mass of new roots if the cuttings have been successful. The shoots can then be cut back to three or four buds above the soil mark and planted out to grow into well-branched young shrubs.

The taking of hardwood cuttings is particularly useful to provide quantities of young shrubs to furnish new borders and thicken up older ones as they are cleared of weeds. Sometimes it may be difficult to find suitable cuttings as short, thin, crowded shoots on old, tangled plants do not root nearly so well as strong shoots from young plants. If a

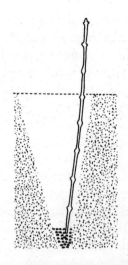

Hardwood cuttings, preferably taken as soon as the leaves have fallen from deciduous plants, provide a ready means of propagating and perpetuating many desirable shrubs. Straight cuttings, prepared from the basal portion of vigorous young shoots with the softer tips removed, are ideal. Rooting powder or liquid will assist the rooting of more difficult plants.

suitable supply is not forthcoming, the parent shrubs should be thinned and pruned hard in the early spring to stimulate strong shoots which can be rooted in the autumn. This pruning, which is likely to be necessary to rejuvenate the garden whether or not cuttings are required, is dealt with in more detail in the next chapter.

Not all shrubs can be propagated in this way, of course. Lilacs and magnolias are virtually impossible; most small flowering trees are very difficult; some roses are easy, others quite impossible; evergreen plants require carefully controlled conditions of high humidity and are best propagated in summer. Despite these difficulties, the approach can be one of 'nothing ventured, nothing gained'. Any shrub which must be pruned or removed can yield a supply of cuttings and if some or all of the cuttings root, well and good.

## DEVELOPING THE GARDEN

Once the mantle of unwanted vegetation has been cleared from the garden it is possible to proceed with development instead of perpetual destruction. Lawns, borders, paths and other features may be marked out and made.

Hose pipe or string are often recommended for marking out curved shapes in gardens but the process is enormously easier if small flower pots or the children's brightly coloured building blocks (subject to their permission) are used. This makes it possible to adjust individual points on the curve with great precision without having to alter the alignment of a continuous hose. I have also used highly visible white polystyrene cups for the purpose but each needs to contain a small stone or they will blow out of alignment even on an apparently perfectly calm day.

### Establishing the lawn and borders

The establishment of a lawn, whether by reclaiming existing vegetation or starting afresh, will mean that a large part of the garden no longer constitutes a perpetual weed problem. Where new borders are planned but cannot be dealt with immediately, these, too, can be sown with grass to improve the soil and mown regularly to prevent weed growth. An even better approach when the garden is to be developed gradually over a period of several years is to sow the grass but to plant the grassed-down borders with bulbs. The grass will then not be cut until midsummer. In this way the contrast of long and short grass gives shape to the garden and the bulbs provide colour;

the effectiveness of border shapes can be judged and altered, if necessary, simply by rerouting the mower, and the taller grass, with its more vigorous root system will improve the soil structure more effectively than would close-mown turf. The effect would be even more attractive if a wildflower meadow mix were used instead of lawn grass seed for the border areas.

As the time for permanent planting approaches the long grass should be mown, as usual, in June or July and again in late September, then sprayed with glyphosate. Regrowth can be sprayed a month later with a third spray, if necessary, early in the new year. Alternatively the close-mown grass can be stripped using a mechanical turf-lifter. If bulbs are to be removed to be used elsewhere they can be dug up as soon as they show through the now-bare soil. The soil should then be in excellent condition for digging and planting. If the bulbs are to remain among the new planting, spraying can be done after the first grass-cut, in July, and again in August in preparation for autumn planting. In this case individual planting holes should be prepared for the shrubs to avoid undue disturbance of bulbs, although most bulbs are remarkably tolerant if replanted as soon as they have been unearthed.

Whether borders are planted at once or after several years of planning and preparation, they should be entirely free of perennial weeds before planting takes place. When established shrubs and trees are to be incorporated in new or rejuvenated borders it may not be possible to clear the whole border. One should then leave a wide band free of new planting around each established plant to allow spot-treatment of recurrent weed problems. Only when the weeds have not been seen for a whole year is it advisable to underplant older shrubs with ground-cover or other low plants.

When planting among existing shrubs it is obviously not possible to dig and enrich the whole border as deeply as might be desired. Much can be done, however, by preparing individual planting holes adequately and top-dressing the whole border with well-rotted compost, manure, or other soil improver and fertilizer. One point on which 'organic' gardeners and 'herbicide' gardeners are in complete accord is in the belief that routine digging, and especially 'forking-over' of borders does more harm than good. Research has shown very convincingly that keeping the soil free of weeds by mulching or spraying leads to much better plant growth than does hoeing or forking.

As soon as the vegetation and surface debris have been cleared sufficiently to allow the outlines of the garden to be determined, work can begin on reconstruction.

## Dealing with unsatisfactory paving

Paving frequently poses a serious problem. Very often in older gardens the barest minimum of hard surface has been put down and in the most haphazard utilitarian manner. A narrow concrete path to the front door, another along the washing line, perhaps a third immediately around the house and two narrow strips for the car is all the paving that many gardens contain, save perhaps a scrap of uneven crazy paving too irregular to take a chair or table. Workmanship is usually poor, and the shoddily laid, cracked and uneven paving is not only dangerous but a conspicuous blemish, no matter how much care is given to lawns and flowers.

Nowadays most people recognize that larger areas of well-constructed paving, clean and simple in outline, form an attractive part of the garden scene. A generous sweep of drive with space for visitors' cars, a broad terrace and ample, well-made paths not only make the garden easy and pleasurable to use but give it a relaxed, expansive character.

It is tempting to conceal inadequate paving beneath new layers of concrete or macadam, but the temptation should be resisted. Unless the area for paving is cleared and evenly consolidated, new paving will quickly settle, sag and crack around old irregularities, so a fresh start is essential.

If large areas of concrete are to be broken up a pneumatic drill will probably be required. Smaller areas can be tackled with surprising ease without mechanical aids if one remembers that concrete is very weak when extended. Rather than banging at the surface with a pick or hammer – causing more sparks than stones to fly – one should excavate a little at the side of the concrete, lever it up with a strong crowbar and then hammer. Broken concrete is not a suitable material for making rock gardens, but it does make quite satisfactory dry walls, or it can be broken into smaller pieces for use as hardcore beneath new paved areas.

When the outlines of the paving are satisfactory but the surface has deteriorated, less drastic measures may be possible. Gravel paths can be resurfaced by removing weeds, leaves, etc., raking up the surface to loosen it then rolling a new layer of gravel into the old. Tarmacadam and asphalt surfaces should have loose material swept off and should be coated with bituminous adhesive before applying a new surfacing layer. Concrete cannot usually be resurfaced: a new concrete skin will quickly crack and separate from the old concrete beneath, while a coating of asphalt will soon show the cracks and irregularities over which it has been laid. If a substantial increase in level can be accommodated, it is possible to spread a 50mm (2in) layer of coarse sand over cracked concrete and to pour new concrete, or to lay precast concrete slabs on top of this. Any unevenness and further movement of the old concrete is then buffered by the sand, but the sand must, of course, be retained at the edges by bricks or concrete or soil, to prevent the new surface collapsing as the sand filters out.

Sometimes areas of unsatisfactory paving have no further use. In this case it is possible to disguise the paving by cracking it (to allow water to drain away) and surfacing with gravel or stone chips, held in place perhaps by a neat trim of bricks with a few large pots of plants for decoration. Even large areas of unwanted paving, such as abandoned tennis courts or redundant drives, may be concealed by trailing or climbing plants. To accelerate the covering, holes may be made within the area and the paving and subsoil removed and replaced by rich soil to receive more plants, but vigorous climbers will cover unwanted paving surprisingly quickly even if planted only on the periphery.

Climbing honeysuckles, including the sweetly scented early and late Dutch, *Lonicera periclymenum*, are especially useful as they are rapid in growth and flower on short laterals which stand up from the surface to give added depth to the carpet. *Vinca major* and *V. minor*, the greater and lesser periwinkles, also spread quickly to form an even, thick carpet of greenery, but they need to be able to root into the soil at intervals so are unsuitable for very large, intact surfaces. Ivies, especially the large-leaved forms, also make handsome, rather flatter, carpets. *Hydrangea petiolaris* is much slower in growth in the early stages but is very attractive in leaf and flower, and in winter its reddish bark glows in weak sunshine. Like honeysuckle it flowers on lateral shoots and will eventually form quite a tall plant even when trailing along the ground.

As always it is important that individual features should form integral parts of the garden: the concealed paving should not look conspicuously like concealed paving but should fit in with the garden. To achieve this aim the area of trailing plants can be extended beyond the limits of the paving, spreading mounds of shrubs used to conceal the edge and perhaps planting holes made within the paving to accommodate tree or shrub groups. Broad patches of several different trailers may be used to break up a large expanse, and paths or clearings may be kept on the old paving for meandering or sitting to enjoy the scene. Swept areas will acquire a carpet of moss while plant-covered areas will soon gather a layer of fallen leaves into which they can root. By use of these and similar techniques an unwanted area of paving becomes a delightful clearing and an integral part of the garden scene.

## Coping with a neglected rockery

Rockeries feature in many older gardens and are very difficult to rescue from neglect. The first step, as with the garden in general, is to remove top-growth to see what lies beneath. In many cases the rockery is of no merit whatsoever: a carpet of ground elder peering from knobbly rubble heaped in a gloomy, damp corner of the garden. If this is so, the rockery can be dismembered and disposed of with no further fuss.

In the rare instance of a rockery which shows some care in its siting, some skill in its construction, some quality in its stone and perhaps some residual interest in its planting, a decision must be made as to whether it is to be reclaimed or demolished. It must be recognized at this juncture that restoring a rock garden is a long-term commitment to painstaking hand-weeding and that a rock garden is not always the best place to grow alpines. Often when a rock garden has become overgrown by 'dwarf' shrubs the most satisfactory treatment is to abandon the idea of a rock garden and to replant with heathers, potentillas, hebes, cistus or other low shrubs more in keeping with the new scale set by the old plants but with enough restraint to allow the rocks to be seen. If, however, a decision is made to keep the rock garden, the next task is selective clearance.

Dwarf conifers and established shrubs should have a zone cleared around them and any branches which have died out because of age or undue shading by weeds should be trimmed off. Lower plants such as saxifrages, campanulas, thrift and other carpeting 'alpines' will have become loose and patchy with age and infested with grasses or perennial weeds. They must be propagated to provide new stock, then the old plants discarded. After the rock garden has been carefully cleared, perennial weeds must be totally eradicated by repeated treatment with translocated herbicide (2-4D or glyphosate). Only when complete eradication is achieved can replanting proceed.

Before planting, the soil should be examined and made good. Most rock gardens, neglected or otherwise, suffer from settling or erosion of the soil, leaving the rocks over-exposed and giving the rock garden a spiky, unsatisfactory appearance. To rectify this, the soil level must be topped up. If the soil appears to be well-drained, gritty and generally in good condition the topping up may be by topdressing only. If the soil has become caked, exhausted and dusty, generous dressings of leafmould or other organic soil improver and coarse sand should be worked in as deeply as possible without disturbing the rocks. If the soil level is still not made good after firming, a further top-dressing of gritty loam can be added. The final appearance should be of a rock mass just visible beneath its thin covering of soil, rather than of a mound of soil with rocks stuck into it.

Planting is a matter for personal preferences. Some gardeners rejoice in a great diversity of alpines, each with its own neatly printed label and segregated from its neighbours by large expanses of stone chips. Others are content to rely on fewer but more generous effects: whole colonies of spring and autumn bulbs and corms spreading and seeding into lawns of thrift, raoulia, thyme and other carpeting plants.

### Treating a neglected pool
Pools are like rock gardens in some respects – very popular in the 1930s they are often to be found in semi-ruinous state by new owners of older houses. Also like rock gardens, when they are good they are very, very good but when they are bad . . . ! The first decision, then, must be on the intrinsic merits of the pool's siting and design. If neither commends itself the pool may be demolished to make way for other features, or, if it is appropriately sited, it may be drained by punching holes in the sides and bottom (assuming that it does not leak sufficiently already), then filled with soil and converted into a bed for plants. It will still tend to hold some water and can be used to grow primulas and other water-loving plants in otherwise dry gardens.

If the pool is to be retained it will almost certainly need to be cleaned and restocked. Despite the obvious discomforts, cleaning is best done in winter or early spring: clearing old ponds in high summer is a good way to lose friends and gain mosquito-bites and will destroy much pond life. Once emptied – by slurry pump or bucket and shovel – the pool should be hosed clean then filled with water. This will determine whether it leaks and the rim is level. If the whole pool has settled so that water runs over one side while the other still has several centimetres of exposed, dry concrete, the higher edge will need to be concealed by trailing and marginal plants.

A steady drop in water level indicates that leaks have developed. Often the water level will drop steadily then remain stable. If refilled it will drop again to the same level, indicating the position of the leak. If the pool leaks it must be emptied, scrubbed free of loose dirt and resurfaced. Waterproofing compounds painted on the concrete may give very satisfactory results but several coats will usually be needed. It is also possible to line the pool with a reinforced butyl liner. These strong, flexible sheets may be obtained cut to size from pool suppliers or in a range of standard sizes from garden centres. They are very easy to install and last indefinitely, but fitting a sheet to the corners of a formal pool is quite difficult.

After the pool has been lined but before it is refilled, soil may be spread over the bottom. In all but the very largest pools, however, it is easier to plant into baskets of soil so that each plant may be encouraged, restricted or moved as required. A week or two after plants, including oxygenating plants, have been introduced, fish and snails may be added to create a balanced and self-maintaining community. Specialist books or catalogues should be consulted for detailed planting suggestions, stocking rates of fish and other information relating to establishment rather than reclamation.

# 4. Tackling Overgrown Plants

Pruning and shaping plants is one of the most important yet least understood aspects of garden maintenance. It is not difficult to understand and once a few simple ideas have been mastered it is among the most rewarding aspects of garden work. Two basic points need to be considered: the ways in which plants grow and the purposes for which plants are used.

To say that plants grow is to state the obvious, but gardeners often overlook the fact that there is no ideal plant. Plants start too small for their situation, grow eventually to the right size and then continue to grow until they are far too large. When the inevitable occurs it is necessary to change the situation, to replace the plant with another small one or to make the plant which is there conform to its situation. The ways in which these changes can be made are described below but first it is necessary to say a little about how plants are used.

## THE PURPOSE OF PLANTS

One distinction of plant use is between utilitarian and ornamental plants, a distinction easily exemplified by comparing a row of Brussels sprouts with a drift of daffodils. In small gardens, though, beauty and utility must be combined and a far more important distinction in those parts of the garden in which appearance is of primary importance is between background and foreground plants. Although one tends to focus on the beauty of individual plants, the success of the garden as a whole depends much more on the arrangement and combination of plants than on individual attractions, so it is useful, in this context, to think in terms of background and foreground, or setting and focal points, or chorus and soloists.

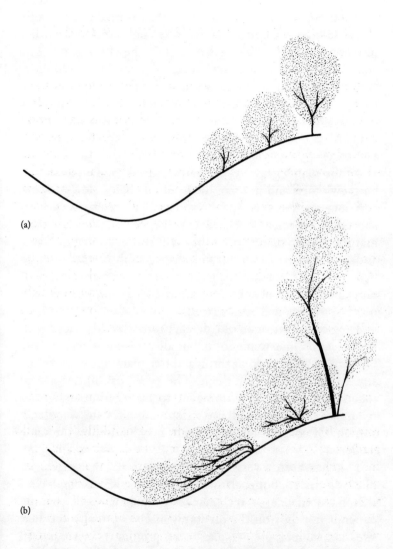

(a)

(b)

Planting designed to emphasize gentle undulations of the ground (a) will
eventually spread to obscure them (b). A peep into any old rhododendron clump
will demonstrate how far plants can travel!

Soloists rely on bright colour or distinctive form or texture for their effect. Too many and the effect is muddled. If individual soloists become too large, too mingled with each other or merged with their background, again the effect is lost. The chorus or background or skeleton of the garden should unite into a single undulating mass, high for screening, shelter or background, low for ground-cover or for framing views or directing the eye. The background planting also shapes and emphasizes open space: lawns, glades, vistas and other important parts of the garden's structure.

As the plants grow, so the garden alters. Some plants will outgrow others and smother them, and if choice, slow-growing and low-maintenance plants succumb to coarse, vigorous, short-lived species, the garden will deteriorate rather than mature. As the plants grow they will spread to engulf lawns and paths and to blur formal shapes. Subtle gradation of heights will be lost and the garden will become an expanse of tall, choked shrubberies hemming in narrow, shaded and poorly-proportioned open spaces.

The new owner of an old, derelict garden will be faced with this situation in extreme form, but all garden owners have the problem of what to do as shrub and tree plantings outgrow the situations intended for them. The two possibilities are to reduce the height by pruning or to burrow into the great mound to make a shaded, mysterious and intimate 'woodland' garden. Of course, both techniques may be used in the same garden.

This has been a very potted and skimpy introduction to planting design, but such a survey is necessary to emphasize that maintenance or reclamation by pruning and shaping depends not only on the plants themselves but also on their situation and purpose. No plant *needs* pruning: plants managed their lives perfectly well for a very long time before humans invented secateurs. It is we humans that *need* to prune plants in order to maximize the benefits we derive from them.

## GROWTH HABITS OF SHRUBS AND TREES

Having looked, albeit briefly, at the purpose of plants, it is now possible to consider the plants, their growth habits and the ways in which these habits can be modified. The four principal types of growth habit are mounded, arching, fastigiate and pyramidal.

Mounded shrubs and trees usually flower at the tips of their shoots, then produce several new shoots, at a wide angle from the old, below the flower head. As these shoots extend, flower and in turn produce new shoots the plant builds up into a rounded mass of fine shoots flowering all over its hummocky surface.

Arching plants may also flower at their tips, but more commonly they flower all along the shoot on short side spurs. New shoots are produced from deep within the plant and, in an effort to reach the light, they grow almost parallel to the older shoots. In youth these plants are stiffly upright. At maturity the shoots are pressed out by neighbours and weighed down by their own extension to produce an arching, vase-shaped outline, in extreme age often arching right over to form a complete dome.

Fastigiate plants are forms which have been selected for the close, upright habit of their many twigs, forming a compact column. Again as the shoots increase in number, length and weight, the column usually becomes broader and less shapely until eventually branches may break out altogether. This habit can be seen in both broad-leaved and coniferous shrubs and trees.

Pyramidal plants are usually conifers. The main shoot produces lateral branches at regular intervals but retains its dominance to grow into a long, unforked, tapering trunk. As the older, lower side-shoots extend, the plant assumes a narrow inverted v shape. Although fastigiate and pyramidal plants appear similar in youthful outline, pyramidal plants do not suffer middle-aged obesity. Sometimes the leading shoot is damaged and two or more laterals grow out to produce new leaders, each with its own separate conical outline. On other occasions the lowest branches of very old trees turn up to make trees in their own right, giving the outward appearance of a colony rather than a single tree.

There are variations on these four forms, of course, and intermediates between them, but once the four basic forms are recognized others are more easily dealt with. In all cases, the objective in pruning and shaping is to control and modify the size of the plant while retaining its natural form. Unless a plant is to be grown as a hedge or piece of topiary, pruning should not distort its natural shape.

### Branch structure

One other important point needs to be mentioned before dealing specifically with the techniques of pruning, and that is branch structure. Mounded, arching and fastigiate plants differ fundamentally from pyramidal plants in this respect. In the first three categories young shoots have the same growth potential as older shoots and lack only their size. In other words it is possible to shorten an old branch back to the point at which a young shoot arises and to know that the new shoot will grow to replace the older one. This technique, which is

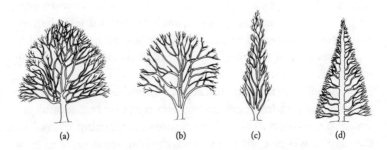

The four principal types of growth-habit –
mounded (a), arching (b), fastigiate (c) and pyramidal (d).

more easily explained by illustration than by words, is known as replacement pruning (see page 116). In pyramidal plants there is only one strong growing shoot. If this is damaged or removed adjacent young growths will eventually take over its role but the shape of the plant will be lost unless all but one of the new leaders are removed while still very small. If a substantial length of leading shoot is removed the lateral branches will very slowly turn upwards and form leaders, but the straight, conical outline will be destroyed. It is therefore extremely difficult to reduce the size of a large, established conical tree and it is usually far more satisfactory to remove it and plant something else.

## PRUNING TOOLS

For most pruning work three, or possibly four, hand tools will be sufficient. Secateurs (or a sharp pruning knife if preferred) will remove twigs and branches up to finger thickness with ease and will deal with larger branches of soft-wooded privet, elder, etc. Longhandled pruners or 'parrot-bills' will tackle heavier shoots very quickly and efficiently. Avoid twisting or levering with these tools: it is bad for the tools and for the plants. A pruning saw with a narrow, curved blade is invaluable for cutting out larger branches from the centre of a shrub as it can be used in very confined situations. A bow saw is quicker and easier when access is not a problem, but a good pruning saw will tackle the same branches more slowly.

As only four items are required it is worth spending money on high-quality tools and taking care of them. It is also worth making life as easy as possible for their user. Dozens or hundreds of cuts may be necessary to bring a single large shrub down to the desired size. Although one or two stout twigs might be tackled with secateurs, after a dozen the wrist and fingers start to register protest – and the secateurs are not improved by the strain. Even though parrot

– bills are a little more cumbersome and need to be put down while twigs are extracted, the benefit to operator and tools after a dozen or a hundred cuts is well worth the extra bother. Similarly, the pruning saw should be used on branches which could just about be tackled by parrot-bills. For very extensive pruning work, hydraulic or powered equipment is available.

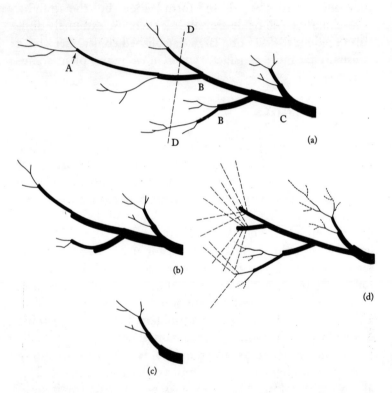

Replacement pruning – the branch shown semi-diagrammatically in (a) could be shortened a little by pruning at 'A', or more severely by pruning at 'B' or 'C'. The effect of pruning at 'B' and 'C' is shown in (b) and (c) respectively. Notice that the natural gradation of the branch from course to fine twigs is retained. Shearing the whole plant, as at 'D', results in unsightly stubs and a mass of uniformly thin twigs (d), ruining the natural shape of the plant.

## PRUNING TECHNIQUES

Cuts must be made carefully. Only when it is necessary to remove an outer layer of twiggery before shaping the main branches can one afford to hack indiscriminately. In all other cases it pays to cut as though this is the final pruning cut, cutting cleanly and close to the branch. When small twigs are removed a single cut is sufficient. If larger, top-heavy branches are to be removed it is advisable to cut several centimetres from the required position to remove most of the weight and then to

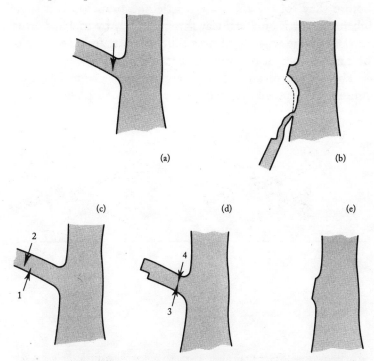

Removal of large branches requires care. Cutting from the top (a) results in the branch tearing away under its own weight (b), leaving a large wound. Undercutting before cutting from the top (c) to remove most of the weight before cutting close to the main branch (d) leaves a clean wound that can be trimmed smooth (e).

finish off with a second cut in the right place. Removing large branches requires four or five cuts: the method is best explained in a diagram (see page 117). There is a raised collar of cells where a branch meets the main stem. The final pruning cut (e) should be as close to this collar as possible without damaging it.

Wood structure varies enormously from plant to plant. When starting on each new plant it is worth cutting off one unwanted branch to 'get the feel' of the plant. Some shrubs and trees have very tough, fibrous wood and will split a long way down the branch if sawn. Others can be cut almost through before they split. Others are brittle and branches will snap when the saw is only half way through. Only by trial and error can one judge where and how much to cut, and the error is best made where it is not important.

The outline of a plant must also be borne in mind when pruning. It is possible to reduce the height of a plant without

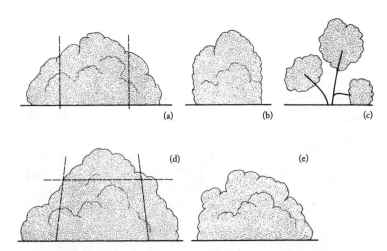

Reducing the spread of a mounded plant without reducing its height (a) leads to an unnatural hedge-like appearance (b), or even to the shrub falling apart (c). A similar reduction in height (d) is required to retain a nicely rounded form (e).

reducing its spread but it is unwise to reduce the spread of a plant without commensurate reduction in height. Narrowing a broadly rounded plant makes it top heavy and liable to take on an unwanted hedgelike appearance, or even to fall apart. The outline proportions are particularly important when trying to curb a wide-spreading horizontal plant such as *Viburnum plicatum* 'Mariesii' or *Juniperus* × *media* 'Pfitzerana'.

## TIMING OF RENOVATION PRUNING

Each of the four seasons has its advantages for pruning work. For regular, light pruning the best time to prune is just after flowering as this leaves the maximum length of time for the plant to produce new flowering wood for the next season. Autumn-flowering shrubs are not usually pruned until early spring.

Late winter or early spring is best for severe renovation pruning as the whole energy of the plant is then directed into new growth. The best time can only be decided in hindsight: advising hard pruning as soon as mild weather is assured is rather like prescribing medicine for a patient to take two hours before he wakes up. If pruning is done too early there is a possibility that any new growth thus stimulated might be killed by subsequent cold weather; if too late, the energy of the plant will already have been directed to top growth which is then cut off, so new growth will be less vigorous and rather delayed. On balance it is better to prune early rather than late.

If very mild weather is followed by exceptionally cold weather there may be damage unless the new growth can be protected by bracken, straw, matting or even the plants' own tops piled upon them.

Summer is a good time to reshape plants by moderate pruning as the shape of the plant in leaf and the effect of pruning on the shape is immediately apparent. By late July or August most plants have stopped growing, so the later in summer reshaping is undertaken, the greater the likelihood is that the invigoration will be directed into the remaining framework of the plant rather than resulting in a rash of new, unwanted shoots around each pruning cut. Late summer is also the best time to cut hedges which are to be trimmed only once each year, as they will then stay tidy for the longest possible period.

Autumn is a time of general clearing up. Pruning in autumn or very early winter allows the plant to compensate for the effects of pruning and to grow normally in spring, producing new and invigorated shoots throughout the plant rather than just around any pruning cuts. There is also time for preliminary healing of cut surfaces before the onset of winter. The disadvantage of pruning after leaf-fall is that the effect is likely to be substantially different when the plant comes into full leaf, and a second pruning may be necessary.

Midwinter is the least desirable time for pruning, both for pruner and pruned, but hardier plants can be dealt with at this time if there is no frost on the plants. A few plants, such as birch, walnut and shrubby cornus, 'bleed' prolifically if pruned at most times of year. There is some debate as to whether the loss of sap is harmful, but certainly it does the plant no good. To avoid bleeding such plants are best pruned in midwinter, not later than mid-January, or else in high summer, August being the best month.

It is not advisable to prune plums, cherries or peaches in winter as the cut surfaces are prone to infection by the silverleaf fungus. Late June, July or early August are the best months for pruning and large wounds are best avoided if at all possible. July and August are also good months in that bleeding, to which some of these plants are also prone, is avoided.

With the exception of these few specific plants, the best time for severe renovation pruning is in March–April and the best time for reshaping is in August–September but, as with most gardening operations, there is considerable flexibility in timing. How it is done matters very much more than when it is done and with a little common sense overgrown plants can be tackled at any time of year.

For many years it was standard practice to seal pruning cuts with bitumen-based tree paint. It is now generally considered that such paints slow the healing process more than they reduce the risk of fungal infection so painting is no longer recommended.

## Pruning overgrown mounded and arching plants

Mounded and arching plants which have grown too large for their situation can be dealt with in one of two ways. Either all the lower branches can be removed and the main trunks thinned to create a picturesque small tree, a new 'soloist', or the overall height of the plant can be reduced until it is satisfactory. In either case always cut back to an outward-facing shoot.

For the first approach, all the thinnest lateral twigs (many of them probably killed by overshading) are removed flush with the larger branches, working upwards from ground level, until

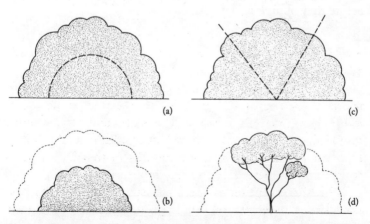

Shrubs which have outgrown their allotted space can either be pruned down (a) to make a smaller mound (b), or pruned up (c) to make a picturesque small tree (d).

A shapeless mound of shrubbery can be given new interest by a
combination of 'pruning down' and 'pruning up'. The new focal
point is displayed against a screening background.

the desired height of the canopy has been reached. The larger
branches can then be removed one by one, remembering that
one can always cut off a branch later if necessary, but a branch
once cut off cannot be stuck on again. As branches are
removed the basic structure of the plant will be revealed and a
clearer picture of the final shape of the plant can be arrived at.
When this shape is achieved it may be necessary to thin the
twiggy canopy a little and it will certainly be necessary to
remove, periodically, new shoots which arise on the main stems
before they obliterate the outline.

A mounded shrub can be reduced in height, often by a third
or more, by carefully removing whole branches back to their
point of origin, with no detriment to the overall shape

If the plant is to be reduced in height the approach again is of cautious 'cut and see', but working from the top of the plant down. Having formed a clear idea of the size and shape required of the plant one can begin by inspecting the tallest part. Trace back along the stem to see where the whole shoot can be removed with minimum detriment to the plant, and cut cleanly above the shoots to be retained. Again it is necessary to work gradually, cutting out quite small pieces and reducing the bulk of the plant slowly.

With care it is often possible to reduce the height of the plant by a third, and its width similarly, without unduly affecting its outward appearance. If further reduction is necessary then still more branches will have to be removed and mounded plants will inevitably assume a rather more open and ragged appearance for a year or two. When the size of the plant must be reduced still further, more drastic measures must be resorted to, cutting back the whole plant to stumps to encourage it to produce a whole new canopy.

Even this apparently simple operation can be done well or badly. Not all plants respond to drastic renovation pruning, so

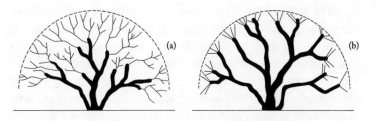

The procedure for more drastic reduction in size, often involving cutting the plant back to bare stumps, is described in the text. It is important to make the final cuts at varied heights throughout the plant and to cut back much further than the ultimate size required. This enables the plant to achieve a natural appearance again (a). Cutting back to evenly and too near the final outline of the plant (b) results in an unnatural mess of twiggy growth with stumps remaining permanently visible.

if there is any doubt, it is advisable to thin the plant as described above and then to wait for new shoots to arise before cutting the plant back further. Usually there will be a few thin, wispy shoots deep within the plant, so old stems can be cut back to these with confidence. When the plant is known to tolerate hard pruning, as with rhododendrons, privets, lilacs, viburnums, laurels and so on, the plants can be cut hard back to a few main branches. Branches should not all be cut back to the same height but should be left well spaced out and with the cut ends arranged at various levels throughout the plant.

It is important to remember, too, that the natural shape of the plant results from large branches near the base becoming progressively finer towards the outside of the plant. Room must be left for this natural gradation to develop, so any large branches which are cut should be cut well below the desired ultimate height of the plant. Cutting large branches back to just within the final envelope of leaves will result in the stumps and masses of thin shoots arising from them being forever visible, spoiling the natural appearance.

Once the shape of the plant is achieved, the finishing touches can be given. Large branches which prove, on careful inspection, to contribute only a few wispy twigs to the outline might be removed entirely. Dead twigs, accumulated leaves and other debris can be cleared away. All cuts should be finished off cleanly and as flush as possible to the branch from which they arise without damaging the all-important collar.

Severe pruning will result in the growth of many strong, straight and un-natural looking shoots. It is important to re-visit severely pruned plants two or three times in the first year after pruning to rub out superfluous shoots and to shorten back others by varying amounts to encourage rapid return to a more natural branching pattern.

Trees can be thinned, shaped and reduced in size in much the same way as recommended for shrubs, but removal of large branches or branches high in the tree is a highly skilled operation and should be left to professional tree-surgeons. Simpler tasks such as the removal of low branches which interfere with mowing, or the reinvigoration of fruiting or flowering trees, are within the abilities of most active gardeners.

## Pruning overgrown fastigiate plants

Fastigiate plants, if they are broad-leaved, are treated just as mounded and arching plants. They can be thinned and shaped like other shrubs and trees except that, to retain the narrow columnar outline, one should prune to an inward-facing new shoot rather than an outwardfacing one. Fastigiate plants are best kept in good shape by regular minor pruning but if after prolonged neglect it is necessary to restore the shape of the plant this is best done by thinning the whole canopy and surrounding it with a sleeve of plastic mesh of the type used for bean netting. Cutting off only outer branches leaves the plant very bare and stumpy at the base. Tying in of wayward branches results eventually in the tied-in branch and the one to which it is anchored being girdled and killed by the tie.

### *Fastigiate conifers*

Fastigiate conifers are those with small, scale-like leaves pressed closely to the branches to create a rather fern-like appearance. The most widely grown are the cypresses (especially Lawson's, Monterey and Leyland cypress) and to a lesser extend, the thujas (especially *Thuja lobbii*). They are quite distinct in form from the needle-leaved, pyramidal conifers (see below) such as pine, spruce, fir, larch and cedar.

Fastigiate conifers are more difficult to deal with, firstly because they do not usually produce new growth when cut hard back and secondly because the dense outer layer of live needles, which give the conifer its attractive colour and texture, conceals a dead brown interior. Any substantial thinning will expose the interior, giving a very moth-eaten appearance. It is sometimes possible to remove whole branches then tie in

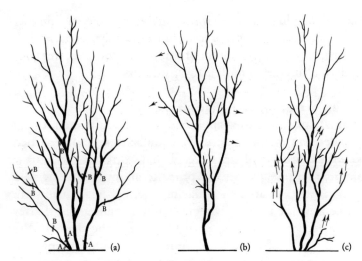

This is a fastigiate (upright-growing) plant (a) that has become rather too broad. Taking off outer branches near their base, as at 'A', leaves a gaunt leggy shrub whose branches will continue to spread as a result of their increasing weight (b). Careful thinning of all the branches, as at 'B', will retain a well-furnished and narrowly columnar shape. Particular attention should be paid to removing long unbranching shoots and shoots with an obvious outward tendancy. Light pruning of vigorous young growth to inward-pointing buds will help to thicken up the shape as indicated by arrows (c).

others to mask the gap thus created, but a much safer technique is to confine pruning operations to the green outer layer of the tree. A surprising amount of growth can be removed by carefully thinning young branches, stopping as soon as any yellow-brown coloration of the inner foliage becomes apparent. The height may also be reduced by taking out the uppermost branches then shaping the remaining tips to re-establish an obvious leading point. Although very few conifers will produce new growth when cut hard back, most will have a few wisps of growth which have not quite been killed out by shading and nearly all will produce more vigorous shoots from the yellowing shoots within the canopy if this is exposed to light by pruning operations. Careful thinning, therefore, will renew the vigour of inner parts of fastigiate conifers, permitting further thinning in successive years and, although it is very rarely possible to make a good small tree out of an unwieldy overgrown fastigiate conifer, it is quite easy to make the tree 'grow backwards', shrinking its size and reshaping it by annual pruning to give the tree a much-extended useful lifespan.

Thujas are much more obliging than the cypresses and will regenerate quite reliably from pruning cuts of 10–30mm (½–1in) diameter or more but an overgrown plant will still take three or four years to regenerate a close mantle of green after severe pruning.

## Pruning overgrown pyramidal plants

Pyramidal plants are the most difficult to deal with as they depend for their elegant shape on the balance between one strong terminal growth and many gradually branching and extending lateral branches. All rules are made to be broken of course, but until one has a great deal of experience with reshaping it is advisable never to attempt to reduce the height of a conical conifer. Cutting out the growing tip will ruin the symmetrical shape. If this growing tip is damaged accidentally, in a storm for example, it is necessary to thin the upper part of the tree to leave one obvious and undisputed new leading shoot, and to tie this to a vertical cane until it shows clear indications of continuing skywards.

The lateral spread of the cone can be limited by careful thinning, as advised for fastigiate trees, and even trees which are known to respond very badly to pruning, such as pines and spruces, can be made to branch and thicken by pinching back the soft new shoots each spring. Each conifer has its own distinctive natural form, however, and there is little which can be done to alter this. Spruces and many pines, for example, lose their lower branches because of self-shading, and spruces in particular become very ragged in middle age. Pines often adopt characteristic picturesque shapes if the dying lower branches are removed, but spruce, including the very popular blue spruce, should be regarded as a temporary plant to be removed when its youthful steel-blue colour fades to dingy grey-green. 'Temporary' here means for a few decades instead of for the few centuries of the plant's natural lifespan, so the problem should not be overstated.

Dwarf conifers are more easily dealt with as they lack the cavernous dead interiors of their larger counterparts. It is worth remembering, though, that most 'dwarf' conifers will outgrow their early 'rock-gardenesque' stature quite quickly. This can be prevented very simply by surreptitious annual snipping which, in many households, will often be done in conjunction with the search for flower-arranging materials.

The best way to deal with overgrown 'dwarf' conifers on a rock garden, assuming the rock garden is to be retained as a feature, is to reveal the often picturesque main trunks by carefully removing the lower branches, thus converting a ground-covering mound of foliage into a diminutive tree. This releases the area beneath the canopy for a carpet of cyclamen or other low, shade-tolerant rock plants. It may be necessary to remove the least attractive conifers completely in order to retain the character of a rock garden rather than of a funereal pine forest.

### Dealing with neglected fruit trees

The question of fruit trees is difficult. Old, unproductive trees may be brought back into bearing by feeding and renewal pruning, gradually opening out the tree and reducing its size to manageable proportions for spraying and picking. Severe pruning will stimulate vegetative growth and it will be two or three years before the tree settles down to flower and fruit again.

If the variety of fruit is not up to the standard required the tree can be top-grafted with a new variety, but this is the subject for a treatise on fruit, of which there are many. The tree may flower well but not fruit, indicating the lack of a polli- nating variety, in which case it is necessary to identify and introduce a suitable pollinator. In many instances the tree may have outlived its useful productive life but if it remains attractive – and few plants can equal a gnarled apple tree for picturesque charm – it should be retained for its appearance alone. Whole orchards can be converted into delightful wild gardens with spring and autumn bulbs and wild flowers in the long grass, perhaps with vigorous roses, clematis or other climbers trained through the trees themselves. Even if any fruit which is produced is totally unfit for human use it will provide an important food source for birds, butterflies and others wildlife.

When it is decided that production is more important than pleasure, a new orchard may be called for. In this case one must remember that fruit trees will not succeed in ground which has been recently cleared of similar fruit trees. Either the orchard must be established on a fresh site or the ground must be well manured and cultivated – perhaps for vegetables – ideally for 5–7 years before replanting with fruit.

### Pruning neglected hedges
Hedges are much more commonly badly maintained than well maintained, and one of the most common problems when taking over an old garden is a large, thin, bulging hedge. Fortunately hedges are by their very nature amenable to pruning, although in the case of coniferous hedges, such as Lawson's or Leyland cypress, this pruning must be confined to new growth. See pages 125–7.

The first step in reclaiming an old, overgrown hedge is to decide on the required size and shape; whether it is to be a tall boundary hedge or a dwarf hedge lining a path or border; whether it is to be a formal wall of greenery or a low, hummocky hedge of lavender or rosemary. Once the outline is determined the hedge must be cut back well within that envelope so that the restored hedge has a thick layer of soft young growth easy to trim to the required shape. A few hedges pose special problems.

Conifers (except *Thuja*) cannot be trimmed into old growth. They can be reduced drastically in height by sawing off the tops of upright branches, but reduction in thickness can only be done very carefully and gradually, as advised for fastigiate trees. It is unwise to tie branches back into the hedge to make it narrower as the ties will be forgotten in a year or two and the branches will be girdled and killed. When reducing the height of a coniferous hedge one should first decide on the outer branches which are to be retained then cut the trunk back to the position from which these branches arise. Simply cutting the hedge straight across at the required height will leave many stumps which will die back and cause problems later on.

Chinese honeysuckle, *Lonicera nitida*, is a popular hedge because of its rapid growth and very low cost, but it is not a good permanent formal hedge. It very quickly becomes full of dead, twiggy growth which looks most unsightly. To restore a small hedge the best method is to take off long young shoots in autumn and root them in a nursery bed, then take out the old hedge, enrich the soil and plant afresh. Alternatively, where there is sufficient room one can simply leave the hedge untrimmed for several years then thin it drastically and allow it to grow again. Chinese honeysuckle is only suitable as a formal hedge if sheared four or five times each year, but as an informal hedge it has a delightful rounded, pendulous shape, turning up at the tips.

Box is an admirable, slow-growing and long-lived hedge but it does not recover well from severe cutting back. If a box hedge has outgrown its allotted size it should first be thinned by cutting out about half of the large branches, thus admitting more light and air to the centre of the hedge. This will result in a rather looser, more open texture than usual but can be done without spoiling the general shape. Thinning and removal of accumulated leaf litter and other debris encourages new growth from deep within the hedge and when this new growth is well established, perhaps after two years, the remaining old growth can be cut back to complete the rejuvenation. The same procedure can be adopted when hebes, heathers and other ornamental shrubs have been used to make small informal hedges.

Most other hedges, privet, hawthorn, beech, hornbeam, yew, holly and laurel for example, can be cut right back to old

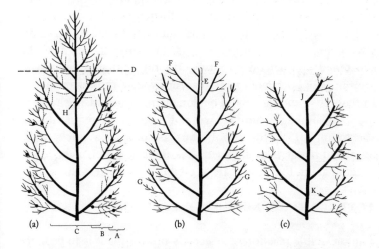

Conifers, such as Lawson's cypress, shown very diagrammatically (a), have an outer layer of young growth (at 'A') concealing an inner yellow layer of dying shoots (at 'B') and a dead, brown centre often choked with debris (at 'C').
Any pruning will reveal the dead interior, so reduction in size is difficult.
Simply lopping at the required height 'D' will result in the situation shown in (b).
The central trunk at 'E', with no green growth to support, will die and decay, causing rot to spread further down the trunk. Top branches 'F' will continue to grow up and out, bowed down by their own increasing weight. Lower branches 'G' will be stimulated by removal of the top, causing the whole plant to develop an unsightly sprawl until it eventually falls apart.
If, instead, the main trunk is cut at 'H' there is no die-back. Living branches at its upper end continue to draw the sap (c). Clearing out dead branchlets and litter at 'J' and shortening side-growths until yellowing shoots are just visible will reduce lateral spread and cause many yellowing shoots to develop new healthy growth as shown by dotted lines in (c). When cuts shown by black dots in (a) have had the desired effect, shown in (c), it will then be possible to reduce the width of the plant still further by cuts such as those at 'K'.

stumps. The thick layer of dry leaves which always accumulates beneath the hedge can then be raked off and the soil top-dressed, if possible, with well-rotted manure or compost. The drastic pruning will result in a mass of new shoots. Privet will usually produce few but vigorous shoots which if left will result in a thin, spindly hedge. These shoots must be shortened by at least two-thirds of their length each spring, or preferably several times each year, to encourage the formation of a dense, firm hedge. Yew and beech will produce numerous little shoots and a few longer, straight, upright shoots. The latter should again be shortened at least once or twice in the first year or two to prevent their continued growth at the expense of weaker shoots. Initially the pruning should be done with secateurs, as shears or mechanical hedge-trimmers will not produce the required even shortening of all the shoots, but as soon as a thick, well-branched hedge is established shearing can begin, using a line or template in the early years to establish the correct shape.

## AFTERCARE OF RESHAPED PLANTS

The inevitable reaction of a severely pruned plant is to produce a mass of new shoots. It is therefore important to follow up initial shaping with further, much less drastic pruning to channel the energy of the plant into useful growth. If new growths are too numerous they may be thinned to perhaps two or three per stem simply by rubbing out unwanted shoots. When no growth is wanted low down on the plant, all the new shoots may be rubbed out, channelling the plants energies into the upper shoots. If the plant is misshapen, perhaps by being crowded before renovation, new shoots resulting from pruning will have a tendency to grow straight up but can be persuaded out and down by tying or weighing them down. Within a year or two the top of the plant will have achieved a new balance with its roots and the only further attention required will be the annual checking of progress.

# 5. Lawn Problems

Before considering the problems associated with lawns it is perhaps advisable to repeat a point made in the Introduction, namely, that this is not intended to be a book dealing with routine cultural practices. Rather its purpose is to explain a little of the background of gardening practice, information usually lacking in traditional gardening books, and to show how this background information helps in the solution of non-routine gardening problems. It is worth making this reminder here because background understanding is of greater importance in turf culture than in any other aspect of garden care.

## HOW A LAWN IS FORMED

Grasses grow from the base of the plant and therefore have their oldest tissue towards the tips of their leaves. Other plants grow from their tips, which become progressively further from the ageing base of the plant as they develop. As a result of this fundamental difference any process, such as grazing, mowing or burning, which removes the top growth of a mixture of plants will favour the grasses, which can continue to grow, and discourage other plants, which thus lose many of their growing points and have virtually to start growing anew. Repeated cropping of a plant mixture will therefore result in grasses becoming the dominant constituents of the mixture. The only other plants which survive repeated cropping of the tops are the very compact rosette plants or trailers which have their growing points very near to ground level.

Repeated mowing, without any other treatment, is sufficient to establish a lawn of sorts and many lawns have been made from rough scrub, brambles or weedy fields simply by repeated mowing. There are, however, a great many grasses, not all of which are desirable lawn grasses, and the quality of a lawn depends on several factors, such as frequency and height of mowing, soil type, degree of shade and climate in general.

## TYPES OF GRASSES

In very wet situations rushes and sedges and vigorous grasses colonize, forming coarse tussocks. Finer grasses fail to flourish and if the 'lawn' is trodden on, the soil quickly loses its structure and finer grasses may die out all together.

On better drained but heavy, fertile soils, rye grass, Timothy and other vigorous agricultural grasses flourish. These can be mown to produce a passable lawn but the grasses are upright and stemmy rather than leafy, so mowing results in a thin turf easily invaded by weeds such as dandelion and buttercup. Worm activity is very great in these moist, fertile soils and worm casts make the soil surface slippery, muddy and prone to further weed invasion.

It is on the lighter, less fertile and more acid soils that the best lawn grasses, the red fescues, bentgrasses and meadow grasses compete most satisfactorily with other plants to produce a short, smooth, fine-textured and bright green lawn. Under such conditions vigorous grasses cannot survive in competition for nutrients with the fine grasses, so they gradually disappear.

If the soil becomes even more impoverished and acid even the bents and red fescues are disadvantaged and they give way to tufted sheep's fescue, wavy hair grass, other stiff tussocky grasses and many low broad-leaved plants, mosses and lichens.

Heavy use of the lawn leads to soil compaction and encourages plantains, daisies, clover and a few other robust plants at the expense of fine grasses. Shade is also very undesirable.

A few grasses and associated broad-leaved plants will tolerate shade but their growth is soft and easily damaged. Close or frequent mowing in shaded areas will quickly cause the grass to fade out, leaving moss and liverwort to colonize the otherwise bare soil.

## ESTABLISHMENT AND RE-ESTABLISHMENT OF LAWNS

To establish a fine, close, weed-free lawn requires not only the right seed mixture but also the right conditions for the new grasses to flourish: an open situation, well-drained, moderately acid soil and frequent, fairly close mowing. Unless one understands and accepts these limitations, a great deal of time and money can be wasted in attempting to establish lawns in quite unsuitable conditions. If a high-quality lawn is considered essential then it is obviously advisable to chose its location with care and to assign any wet or shady situations to other types of plants. On heavy soils it will be necessary to import large volumes of sand or other free-draining growing medium.

It is important to remember that removing the top of a grass plant also restricts the development of its roots. Very close-mown lawns will have very shallow root systems and will be very prone even to short periods of drought. A very fine lawn will need not only frequent mowing (every day for the close green baize of a bowling green – including Sunday) but very careful attention to levelling, feeding, irrigation and drainage. Simply raising the height of mowing from green baize to bedroom carpet or deep pile rug will, at a stroke, simplify all other aspects of lawn care.

Increasingly, therefore, gardeners are adopting less rigid definitions of what constitutes a good lawn. While there are some situations in which a close, green velvet carpet is appropriate, there are many others in which lawn 'weeds' – from the humble daisy to delicate orchids and harebells – are not only acceptable but desirable 'wild flowers'. Indeed the establishment of grass areas of different heights and characters is one of the easiest and most interesting ways of achieving variety of effect in a large garden. If grass and lawns are viewed in this context, re-establishment of a lawn and the solving of lawn problems become very much easier.

As mentioned at the beginning of this chapter, close regular mowing will result in a lawn being formed regardless of the original vegetation. A robust rotary mower or flail will be necessary to tackle coarse scrub and brambles but after two or three passes of the machine at intervals of several months the woody growth will begin to give way to softer vegetation and within a couple of years an acceptable rough lawn will be produced. This could then be mown every two or three weeks with a rotary or gang-mower, or left long to reap the benefit of wild flowers, introduced bulbs and so on, then cut two or three times in the late summer. Where bulbs are not planted it is also possible to mow the grass a few times in April–May and then to leave it to grow as an attractive summer meadow. Any remaining coarse weeds such as docks or thistles will need to be spot-treated with lawn weedkiller.

## IMPROVEMENT OF THE LAWN

### Levelling the lawn

If a finer lawn is required, more frequent and closer cutting with a domestic rotary or cylinder mower will be necessary. The closer the lawn is cut, the more essential is a level surface. Small undulations which are quite insignificant when the mower is passing 75–100mm (3–4in) above the surface become of major importance as the cutting height is reduced to 15mm (½in) or less. Hollows are insufficiently cut and collect water so they become a thick, rich green, while hillocks are shaved of grass and become dry and brown, creating an unsightly, patchy lawn.

Undulations may be corrected by rolling back the turf and removing or adding soil to make the level true, but this requires considerable skill if the end result is not to be more hummocky than the original lawn. An easier method, satisfactory in many situations, is to remove soil from high spots, with a hollow-tine turf-spiker, and to use this soil, suitably pulverized, to brush into hollows. Used as recommended for turf aeration hollow-corers have little effect on soil level, but if used repeatedly at close spacing on high spots they can result in a useful lowering of soil level. Foot-operated tools can be used for small areas but the work is very tiring and a hollow-coring machine will be necessary for large areas. These are expensive but can be hired as required.

The smooth, close lawn which results from levelling and weekly low mowing will be sufficient for large lawns. In small gardens where evenness of colour is more critical it may be necessary to improve the quality of the lawn still further by the use of fertilizers, weedkillers and perhaps over-seeding.

### Lawn fertilizers

Obviously there is not much point in applying expensive weedkillers to improve a lawn if there is little grass left when the weeds have been killed. When the sward consists mainly of daisies, hawkweeds, clovers, moss and lichen with very little grass, indicating an impoverished condition, it is advisable to feed the lawn for a season before attempting to control the weeds. Proprietary brands of lawn fertilizer have instructions for use printed on the bags, but for turf reclamation the maxim should be 'little and often'. Half the recommended rate of fertilizer, apportioned in three doses for April, June and September, will encourage grasses to grow more vigorously without so encouraging the weeds that any remnant of grass is choked out. Once grass has begun to grow well, you can turn to more direct control of weeds.

## Lawn weedkillers

Hormone weedkillers based on 2-4D and closely related compounds revolutionized weed control in lawns in the second half of the twentieth century. They act by overstimulating the weeds which become grossly distorted and then die. Such weedkillers are therefore most effective if applied when growth is already rapid, in warm wet weather and preferably after fertilizer application. May (if warm) and early June (if moist) are ideal months for treatment. Some weeds are more resistant than others to the various hormones, so it may be necessary to use several applications of more than one weedkiller to effect a complete kill, if that is the aim, but a single application of any type is enough to achieve a marked improvement in the quality of the lawn.

### Lawn sand

The availability and ease of use of hormone weedkillers, which have only to be diluted and watered onto the lawn, have led to the neglect of lawn sand as a means of controlling weeds. This is unfortunate as, although it is less convenient and less rapid in its effect, lawn sand has several advantages, acting as a weedkiller, a fertilizer and a soil conditioner simultaneously to produce a gradual but long-lasting improvement in lawn quality.

Lawn sand consists of 3 parts sulphate of ammonia, 1 part sulphate of iron and 20 parts sand or finely screened soil to facilitate even distribution. It can be bought ready-mixed or made up at home and can be applied at $120–180g/m^2$ $(4–6oz/yd^2)$, two or three times a year if required, when the weather is warm and dry.

It acts by settling on, and therefore scorching, broad-leaved and horizontal growing plants, such as daisies, plantains, cat's ear and even the coarser grasses, while sifting down harmlessly among the finer grasses. Sulphate of ammonia is, of course, a potent fertilizer, so it stimulates grasses to grow into the spaces left by scorched weeds while the acid reaction of sulphate of ammonia lowers the pH of the soil, which again favours fine grasses at the expense of coarser vegetation. Sulphate of iron is an effective moss-killer (whereas hormone weedkillers have no effect on moss except to provide it with more bare spaces to colonize) and produces a rich, dark green colour in the turf, while the sand or fine soil used as a spreader has a beneficial effect in keeping the lawn surface open and well drained.

*Other weed control measures*
Slitting and raking the lawn will discourage trailing and broad-leaved weeds in favour of fine grasses. Hand-operated or mechanically-propelled equipment can be obtained for both operations. Alternatively mower attachments will allow two jobs to be done simultaneously.

Mowing itself will help to control weeds. Raising the mowing height will allow grasses to grow more vigorously thus forcing the growing points of weeds up to where they are more readily removed by the mower. Indeed, the combination of nitrogenous fertilizer to stimulate grass and increasing the mowing height to allow this vigour to be expressed will steadily improve the lawn even without the use of weedkillers. The disadvantage, of course, is that stimulated grass must be mown more frequently than impoverished grass but this is a problem which must be faced if a perfect lawn is required.

## Over-seeding the lawn
Although creation of the right conditions for a lawn will eventually result in a fine lawn being produced as the appropriate grasses invade and colonize, the process is much speeded up by deliberate introduction of these desirable grasses. One way of doing this is to resow the lawn entirely, a process which is described later. The other method is to introduce seed of the desirable grasses into an existing sward by over-seeding. The results are less certain and less spectacular than remaking a

lawn in its entirety, but there are many instances in which the technique of over-seeding is entirely appropriate.

If a lawn has been made by constant mowing of coarse vegetation it may be reasonably level and an even green when viewed from a distance, yet too patchy on close inspection, being composed of dandelions, buttercups, coarse tufty grasses and thistles, with many bare patches. The work of killing weeds, cultivating the soil, reestablishing a firm, level surface, then sowing a new lawn is very considerable, and the new lawn cannot be walked on for several months. In such cases, over-seeding is an ideal method of improving the lawn.

The work begins with fertilizer application in April, to stimulate growth, then treatment with hormone weedkiller in June when the grass is growing most vigorously. This will kill most of the coarse weeds, leaving rather more bare patches than usual. By August the lawn will be ready for scarifying, or vigorous raking, to tear out any dead vegetation and loosen the soil surface. After one more mowing and a further loosening of the soil the grass seed can be applied at $15-30g/m^2$ or $\frac{1}{2}-1oz/yd^2$ (the heavier rate for seed mixes containing rye grass). Ideally the seed should be applied in a top-dressing of finely sifted compost. If this is not possible the seed should be raked gently to cover it with soil. Regular mowing must now cease, but by mid- or late September the new grass will have grown sufficiently to warrant a light rolling, followed, a week or so later, by mowing with the mower set as high as possible. There will usually be time for three or four more mowings before winter sets in and the grass should be topped during the winter if mild, dry weather permits. In the following year grass maintenance can begin as usual and by September the new part of the lawn will be sufficiently well established to permit careful use of weedkillers if necessary. In the following years weed eradication can begin in earnest, in the knowledge that there is sufficient fine grass to replace the weeds as they are killed.

## Aeration of the lawn

Another effective method of improving turf, especially old and obviously impoverished lawns, is by aeration. This can be done by slitting or by hollow-tining, using equipment bought or hired for the purpose. Slitting chops up trailing plants such as clovers and yarrow, thus favouring the development of fine grasses. Hollow-tining removes cores of soil to improve air and water penetration through the compacted surface.

The holes left by hollow-tining can be filled with sand and fertilizer or with fine compost to improve drainage and nutrition simultaneously. For even more beneficial effect, hollow tining can be followed by brushing in top-dressing mixed with grass seed, a combination of aeration and over-seeding in one operation.

### REMAKING A LAWN

If the level is reasonably even and obstacle-free, much can be done to improve existing lawns. Old, worn-out lawns can be improved by scarifying, applying fertilizers, judicious use of weedkillers and increasing the mowing height as described above. Coarse meadow or scrub can be improved by close mowing, weedkillers and over-seeding. There are situations, however, when a fresh start is advisable. The ground may be very uneven, deeply rutted or littered with stumps or the situation may require immediate installation of a fine lawn.

The first operation should be a complete kill of perennial weeds by application of glyphosate and the removal of any stumps and other obstacles. Next any major levelling will be done taking care not to mix topsoil and subsoil. With care it is possible to produce a lawn on subsoil only, but an uneven depth of topsoil as a result of haphazard levelling operations will result in a permanently uneven, and therefore unsatisfactory, lawn. Surface cultivation follows levelling to produce the required fine soil for sowing of seed. If major relevelling is not necessary, it is advisable to cultivate only deeply enough to remove the minor irregularities and to produce a fine surface in which to sow. Deep cultivation is not only expensive of time, money and energy but often results in deterioration of soil structure and in long-term settlement causing unevenness of the surface.

After the surface has been levelled, firmed and raked, seed sowing can proceed as recommended in any of the innumerable books on lawns, in leaflets issued by lawn seed suppliers or, very briefly, in the section above dealing with over-seeding.

For even quicker results turf can be used but it is more expensive. It is very important to buy high-quality lawn turf. Poor-quality, uneven, weedy turf stripped with a minimum of preparation from building sites or meadows is worse than useless. If turf is to be used, it must be obtained from a reputable source, preferably after inspecting samples.

## COPING WITH SOME COMMON LAWN PROBLEMS

The brief survey of lawn renovation and establishment above indicates the solution to many lawn problems but it is worth picking out a few of the more common difficulties which have not already been mentioned specifically, to see how they might best be dealt with.

### Moss on lawns

Moss invasion may indicate a whole range of problems. There are nearly as many mosses as there are grasses, with different mosses invading in different situations, but only when conditions are in some way unsuitable for grass growth will mosses become a problem. The soil may be impoverished, too acid, too dry, too wet or too shaded to support closely mown turf and in each case mosses will invade. The solution, obviously, is to remedy the situation: there are several proprietary chemical treatments for moss but, although effective in killing the existing moss, they will not prevent its reappearance.

Aeration of the lawn and fertilizer application are helpful in many cases and increasing the mowing height by a notch or two of the mower adjustment will improve the vigour of the grass and help it to out-complete the moss. These treatments are especially beneficial on thin, impoverished turf.

## Excessively acid lawns

When the moss is in large, dark green patches on an old lawn with very low, thin turf and bare soil patches, which crack and flake off in dry spells, the soil is almost certainly too acid. Although fine grasses require a slightly acid soil (pH 6 or 6.5 is ideal), excessive acidity will discourage grass, destroy soil structure and encourage mosses. Acidity can be checked with a soil-testing kit and rectified by cautious application of lime, bearing in mind that if liming is overdone, coarse grasses and worms will be encouraged. $30–70g/m^2$ ($1–2oz/yd^2$) of ground chalk or limestone is preferable to quicker-acting hydrated lime and should be applied in autumn or winter, with a second application a year later if tests indicate that the soil is still too acid. Alternatively, as excessive acidity is frequently associated with soil impoverishment, it is possible to use a fertilizer with an alkaline reaction: nitrochalk is ideal for this purpose, applied in spring or early summer at $15–30g/m^2$ ($½–1oz/yd^2$). Sulphate of ammonia, which is acid in reaction, should be avoided as a fertilizer on excessively acid soils.

## Dry lawns

Dry lawns occur on light, sandy soils. In many respects these soils are ideal for lawns, but the grass browns in dry weather. No permanent harm is done: the grass recovers its colour within days of rain falling and many weeds are affected even more seriously by drought, so the lawn may even be improved. Clover and yarrow remain bright green, however, and this results in a patchy appearance. When it is desired to keep the grass greener for longer the soil must be made more retentive and more fertile. A mixture of organic soil improver and fertilizer can be used for this purpose as a top-dressing, but it is much more effective if it can be worked into the surface after hollow-tining. The improvement is thus effected below the immediate surface and grass roots continue to benefit after the surface itself has dried out. Nitrogenous fertilizers are most immediately effective, but phosphate, which is often lacking on light, acid soils, will stimulate root action and result in long-term improvement.

Annual treatment over several years will produce a stronger, more drought-resistant turf, but close mowing and surface applications of fertilizer and peat will encourage roots to develop only in the surface soil where they are very quickly affected by drought. Irrigation will, of course, prevent browning of the turf but application of water should be infrequent and thorough to stimulate deeper rooting.

## Muddy lawns
There are three causes for muddy, slippery lawn surfaces: compaction, worm activity and heavy soil.

### *Compaction of the lawn surface*
When the lawn surface has been compacted by heavy use or by mowing with heavy machinery, root activity decreases, soil-structure deteriorates and water fails to penetrate. Even when the soil below is light and freely drained, the surface then becomes wet and slippery in rainy weather. To overcome surface compaction the holy trio of spiking to improve drainage and fertilizer plus sand application and increasing mowing height to improve root activity can be employed.

If the compaction is localized because of well-worn paths to the vegetable plot, to the shed or between closely planted trees, it may be advisable to install a proper path, or at least to alter the mowing regime as described below, in the section on patchy lawns.

## Worm casts on the lawn

Worm activity results in many casts being produced on the surface. These cones of fine soil become trodden or flattened by the mower, resulting in a slippery, wet surface ideal for moss and weed invasion. Cast-forming worms are discouraged by acid soil conditions, so the use of ammonium sulphate as a fertilizer or lawn sand as a weedkiller will not only improve the soil for fine grasses but will also discourage worms. There are also proprietary compounds for expelling or killing worms but the consequences are not entirely beneficial.

Worms play a major role in improving soil structure and surface drainage as well as dragging dead leaves into the soil. Eradication of worms may lead to poor drainage and the accumulation of mowings and dead grasses as a surface thatch, problems which cannot entirely be remedied by additional hollow fining and scarifying.

## Lawns on heavy clay soil

Muddy conditions caused by heavy clay soil pose a more serious problem. Fine grasses are not well adapted to clay, coarser grasses which grow well on clay are not well adapted to close mowing, so attempts to produce a close lawn are bound to result in thin, patchy turf riddled with worm casts, wet and mossy in winter and cracked in summer.

To create a good lawn on clay it is necessary to modify the soil deeply with coarse sand, crushed clinker and organic material in large quantities and to ensure that the lawn is freely drained, not situated in a hollow in which the underlying clay will hold water. For a tennis court or other playing surface it is standard practice to remove the topsoil, lay tile drains, cover the whole site in coarse sand or shingle then to sow the grass on a shallow layer of topsoil over this freely drained base. Any less elaborate treatment is inadvisable if a firm, level, well-drained and resilient surface is essential.

Such preparation are hardly necessary for a domestic lawn, however, if one accepts a deeper lawn. Grass is one of the most effective soil improvers, as anyone who has walked across thick grass on to bare soil in winter will appreciate, but grass roots will only develop effectively if a reasonable amount of top growth is left on. On clay soil it is advisable to establish an effective system of dry paths so that the grass need not be trodden on in wet weather and to cut the grass at 40–50mm (1½–2in) height instead of the customary 10–15mm (½in) or less. Very short grass is an English tradition, not a necessity, and a long but even sward is more effective than a short patchy one. On a large lawn the grass could be cut even higher, perhaps 100mm (4in) long, at which height it will ripple beautifully in the breeze. Alternatively, the grass may be left very long with spring and autumn bulbs, and mown only two or three times in late summer. This treatment is suitable for large or small gardens as long as it is evident, from the shape and treatment of the 'meadow', with paths mown around and through it, that the long grass is a deliberately planned part of the garden and not merely a result of neglect.

**Patchy lawns**
Very seldom is the grass uniform throughout a garden. Small scale patchiness resulting from weeds, diseases, surface irregularities and similar problems has been dealt with already, but the grass also varies on a larger scale as a result of varying conditions. Thin, dry soil, on steep banks, dry, shady conditions under trees, worn grass along major routes in the garden, damp, shady areas near walls or buildings all result in different types of grass and different responses of grass to an overall uniform maintenance regime. Trees where birds gather or roost, such as cherries or mulberries, have lush, dense grass as a result of bird droppings. It is possible, by adjusting fertilizer, irrigation, aeration, mowing and other cultural practices to create a more or less uniform turf despite varying conditions,

but a far more satisfactory approach is to use these natural variations as the basis of the garden's design.

Large trees which shade the ground or groups of small trees which interfere with mowing can be set in areas of long grass and bulbs: daffodils and snowdrops in moist places; anemones, aconites and cyclamen in dry. These islands of longer grass emphasize the presence of the trees at ground level. Banks and shaded areas, too, can be mown longer and less frequently or, where grass growth is very poor, replaced entirely by other ground-cover plants. The greater part of the remaining lawn could be mown at an intermediate height suitable for rough use, while well-worn tracks and the most formal areas of lawn will be closely mown and intensively managed or reinforced by stepping stones. The variation needs to be worked carefully into a design, of course. Little circles of long grass around individual apple trees look unkempt; six strips of grass of different heights and textures in a small garden look fussy and are tedious to maintain.

There is now a great variety of equipment for lawn maintenance. There is a growing realization that a variety of effects is possible. Although grass maintenance is readily mechanized it is still one of the most time-consuming aspects of garden maintenance and if one learns to work with natural variations rather than against them, to capitalize on the variety, the effect can be simultaneously more satisfying and less expensive in time and materials.

# 6. Summary and Postscript

Throughout these pages it has been emphasized repeatedly that this does not claim to be a complete gardening book – far from it. There is a welter of publications already dealing with straightforward aspects of soils and manures, pests and diseases, plant propagation, pruning, lawn care and other routine aspects of garden cultivation, and new books are added to the list almost every day.

The aim of this book has been to deal with particularly difficult or non-routine problems and to deal with them in such a way that they may first be understood and then, as a result of this understanding, more easily overcome. Very often a 'problem', on careful consideration, turns out to be not a problem at all but an indicator of the best way to develop a garden.

The emphasis throughout has been on working within constraints, rather than overcoming them, to produce a garden appropriate to the situation by 'consulting the genius of the place'. It has been interesting to watch developments of recent years in other aspects of life and to observe that, as a result of pollution scares, oil crises, droughts, soaring costs and other hazards of modern civilization, even highly sophisticated or rigidly traditional societies and institutions have adopted the more pragmatic, creative or 'ecological' approach recommended here.

The range of problems has, I hope, been sufficient to meet most situations, but two more topics remain to be discussed – maintenance of large gardens and sources of further information.

## MAINTENANCE OF A LARGE GARDEN

The upkeep of large gardens is a subject for a book in itself, but it has been touched upon in many places throughout this book. Large gardens pose particular problems but they also have special advantages. Because of their size, simplicity of effect is very desirable; concentration of seasonal effects in particular parts of the garden is possible and both simplicity and specialization simplify the use of mechanical and perhaps chemical aids.

Large gardens usually have a legacy of wide paths, steps and terraces all of which can now be maintained very easily with a range of modern equipment.

The major part of the garden will usually be devoted to lawns. Again much assistance is available, not only for mowing but for aerating, scarifying, leaf-blowing and sweeping – any job which is likely to need doing. Although easily mechanized, maintenance is still time-consuming, especially if there are large areas of fine lawn which need to be mown every week. This need not be so, of course – the last chapter dwelt very heavily on the advantages of abandoning traditional concepts of lawn maintenance in favour of a more creative and more environmentally sensitive approach.

The greater the height of cut, the less often grass needs to be mown and the less other maintenance is required. Fine bowling greens must be mown two or three times each week but preferably every day. A good lawn maintained at 15mm (½in) high will require mowing once each week at least. At 40–50mm (1½–2in) high, mowing every 10–14 days is ample and with truly long grass three mowings in July/August/September will be sufficient, with one mowing each year adequate for some situations. Annual mowing takes longer than a single weekly mowing, of course, and requires different equipment, but the job is not a regular commitment and can be fitted into the least busy time of year in the best weather conditions.

The overall appearance is better if longer, more natural areas are large in relation to fine lawns and establishment of ornamental meadows or orchards of flowering or fruiting trees in long grass will result in very substantial savings in time over the year, especially as it is often the more difficult areas – steep banks or areas of scattered trees – which are mown less often.

Some of the time saved by varying lawn maintenance can be used to revitalize borders. Again large gardens often have the advantage of old, established shrubs which are resistant to carefully applied herbicides. The ground beneath these shrubs may be left bare for ease of herbicide application, or planted with ground-cover plants, or a combination of both. Bare ground soon becomes attractively moss-covered and may be planted with spring bulbs depending on the extent of weed invasion.

Mature evergreen shrubs are themselves effective ground-covers but where the situation is light enough to encourage annual weed growth, mulching with bark chips or other clean organic soil improver will greatly reduce the effort of weeding and enhance the growth of desirable plants. Small bulbs will not push through a thick layer of mulch so, where the simple effect of shrubs in a mulched surround would be too bland, ground-cover planting may be employed once the area has been freed of any perennial weeds.

Ground-cover planting need not mean large tracts of *Hypericum calycinum* or ivies, attractive though these may be in some situations. The possibilities are endless and one can not do better than to read the classic book on *Plants for Ground Cover* by Graham Thomas, first published by Dent in 1970 and most recently by Timber Press in 1990), or Margery Fish's delightful *Ground Cover Plants* (Collingridge, 1964; Batsford, 2002). These have extensive lists of plants and, even more important, an excellent introduction to the principles and practices of using ground-cover plants.

## SOURCES OF FURTHER INFORMATION

The mention of Graham Thomas's book leads naturally to other sources of information. The combination of principle and practice makes *Plants for Ground Cover* one of the holy trilogy on my bookshelf. The others are his *Perennial Garden Plants* (Dent, 1990, republished by Frances Lincoln in 2004) and a much-battered *Hillier's Manual of Trees and Shrubs*. Both of these are excellent reference sources but are especially valuable for their extensive lists of plants suitable for particular soils and situations. The combination of principle and practice which makes *Plants for Ground Cover* so useful is also found in Lawns by R.B. Dawson, published by Penguin and the Royal Horticultural Society in 1960. It is long out of print but still to be found in second-hand bookshops.

The Arboricultural Association, based at Ampfield House, Romsey, Hants SO51 9PA, is a useful source of advice on trees and tree care. Of particular use are the booklets on selection, care and protection of trees, and trees and the law, but the Association also maintains a register of qualified tree surgeons to whom one might turn for advice on particular problems. The register, and other information on the Association, is also available on-line at www.trees.org.uk.

The British Association of Landscape Industries also maintains a register of its members and publishes a list of its members, region by region, with an indication of the scope of their work. By this means it is possible to locate local firms well qualified to undertake landscape construction, maintenance and design work. The register is available from BALI, Landscape House, Stoneleigh Park, Warwickshire CV8 2LG or www.bali.co.uk.

The Institute of Horticulture booklet 'Education and Training Courses' (from the Secretary of the IoH, 14/15 Belgrave Square, London SW1X 8PS, or www. horticulture.org.uk) is not intended for locating sources of gardening advice as such but it does list all the horticultural courses offered in Britain and therefore contains addresses of many colleges and the few universities throughout Britain with staff who may be able to offer advice.

The Royal Horticultural Society, which has published many other useful and inexpensive small books since the Penguin series, is in itself the most useful source of information for gardening enthusiasts. Members of the Society are able to obtain expert advice on all manner of gardening matters from the staff at Wisley, to use the marvellous library at Vincent Square, to receive the monthly journal *The Garden* which is increasingly full of useful ideas, and to visit the Society's gardens at Wisley (Surrey), Rosemoor (Devon), Hyde Hall (Essex) and Harlow Carr (Yorkshire), themselves as useful as a whole library of books. Information on membership may be obtained from the Secretary at Vincent Square, London SW1P 2PE or from its website www.rhs.org.uk.

Professional design is more the province of the garden designer or, usually for larger schemes only, the landscape architect than of the landscape contractor. Lists of consultants may be obtained from the Society of Garden Designers, Katepwa House, Ashfield Park Avenue, Ross-on-Wye, Herefordshire HR9 5AX (www.sgd.org.uk) or the Landscape Institute, 33 Great Portland Street, London W1W 8QG (www.landscapeinstitute.org).

All these organizations are national in scope but much help can be gained locally from horticultural societies and other amateur groups. The town hall or central library often maintains lists of societies. Alternatively, an enquiry at a local flower show or adult education centre will quickly produce the required address.

Lastly, but certainly not least, there is no better or more enjoyable way of learning about one's own garden than visiting other gardens, far or near. Local papers advertise open days of nearby gardens, but the annual list published by the National Gardens Scheme is an excellent investment. *The Yellow Book* is available each spring from booksellers or, in case of difficulty, from the National Gardens Scheme, Hatchlands, East Clandon, Guildford, Surrey GU4 7RT (www. ngs.org.uk).

# *Index*